INDEPENDENT COMMISSIONS

IN

THE FEDERAL GOVERNMENT

INDEPENDENT COMMISSIONS

IN

THE FEDERAL GOVERNMENT

BY WILSON K. DOYLE, PH.D.

CHAPEL HILL

THE UNIVERSITY OF NORTH CAROLINA PRESS

1939

TO

MY MOTHER AND FATHER

Preface

IN GOVERNMENT, as in private life, there is a tendency to stereotype methods of action or methods of conduct. Things begun in a spirit of innovation, if they do not work altogether badly, often become not merely approved methods of action but final criteria. For a long time substantially this attitude existed with respect to the independent commission. But, fortunately, there is today a tendency to question it as a final type of governmental technique. Indicative of this tendency is the recent report of the President's Committee on Administrative Management, to which this study was submitted while in manuscript form.

My thanks are due especially to Dr. James Hart for his invaluable criticism and guidance. His encouragement and scholarly example have been a source of genuine inspiration.

W. K. D.

Contents

INDEPENDENT COMMISSIONS

IN

THE FEDERAL GOVERNMENT

CHAPTER ONE

Introduction

IN STUDIES of the federal government the term "independent commission" has been generally used to identify certain agencies which are considered parts of the administrative framework because of their administrative powers and which are organized under a board control and generally regarded as independent of the president. The extent to which these agencies are actually in a position to function as independent units is later examined. The word "independent" is used in this work simply for identification.

Though all of these agencies are entrusted with administrative powers, many are also entrusted with policy formulating and judicial powers. By administrative powers are meant those minor discretionary tasks of government which involve merely the function of carrying into execution governmental programs including, where some form of legal proceedings becomes necessary, the function of instituting the proceedings and representing the public therein.[1] By policy formulating powers are meant those tasks in which discretion is so broad as to involve the actual formulation in whole or in part of the direction or objectives of governmental programs. The term is used in place of legislative powers because in most cases these commissions are required to exercise their policy formulating powers by specific orders instead of by

---

[1] The term is used synonymously with executive powers in this study.

general regulations.[2] Basically, the distinction between policy formulating and administrative power is the distinction between power in respect to objectives of social and economic policy and power simply in respect to methods. But the only practicable test is the degree of discretion entrusted. For, however the power of a particular agency may in theory be restricted to method only, it invariably becomes a power in respect to objectives if sufficient discretion is entrusted. It is recognized that such a test may lead to differences of opinion in borderline cases.

The term judicial power, as used in this study, has no procedural implications. Hence any power which involves some measure of legal finality in the decision of controversies respecting the rights of individuals or parties is classified as judicial power regardless of whether the power is exercised according to the general procedure of a court.[3] Since administrative power, as earlier defined, involves the application of policy to specific individuals or parties, its exercise may frequently result in a final decision of the rights of specific individuals or parties. This will occur when the individuals in question do not dispute the administrative decision. But if they do dispute the decision, if, in short, a controversy exists, and if the ordinary courts will recognize the right of the administrative agency to a measure of legal finality by refusing to review and redetermine the issue in whole or in part, the administrative decision then becomes an exercise of judicial power.

In the instances where Congress has denied these commissions policy formulating and judicial powers, their administrative powers are necessarily performed as a distinct function. But, where it has also entrusted them with policy formulating or judicial powers or both and required them to proceed for the most part by specific orders, their administrative powers are for the most part combined with their other powers into one action.

---

[2] The term quasi-legislative is most commonly used to identify this power.

[3] The term quasi-judicial is most commonly used to identify this power.

The most important commissions and the ones with which this study is concerned are the following: the Interstate Commerce Commission, the Federal Communications Commission, the Securities and Exchange Commission, the Federal Power Commission, the Federal Trade Commission, the National Bituminous Coal Commission,* the National Labor Relations Board, the United States Maritime Commission, the Board of Governors of the Federal Reserve System, the Employees Compensation Commission, the Social Security Board,* the National Mediation Board, and the United States Tariff Commission.

The purpose of this study is to discuss certain broad institutional aspects of these commissions. Specifically it will discuss: (1) the present sources of presidential influence which serve to undermine complete independence of action; (2) whether, in fact, independence and also board control, which is another feature of commission organization, seem likely to result in the most effective performance of the work assigned to these commissions; (3) whether the combination of powers now entrusted to most of these commissions and the procedure which most of them are required to follow, seem likely to result in the most effective exercise of these powers.

An examination of the powers entrusted to these commissions and the procedural requirements shows five somewhat different purposes for which the independent commission is being used. The first and most common use being made of the independent commission is for the exercise, by a process of adjudication for the most part, of policy formulating and judicial powers in conjunction with administrative powers. In this process of adjudication they are required to proceed much as a court with formal notice and hearing accorded the individuals or parties whose

* Since this was written the National Bituminous Coal Commission has been abolished and its functions assigned to a subordinate single head agency, the Department of the Interior. Also, the Social Security Board has been made a subordinate unit in the newly created Federal Security Agency, a single head agency which is apparently altogether subordinate to the President.

rights are being adjudicated. Their policy formulating and administrative powers are thus exercised in large part in the process of adjudicating the rights of individuals or parties. At the same time, however, they have also the administrative responsibility for initiating action or complaints leading to adjudication when necessary in the public interest, so that their judicial powers extend to many controversies in which they themselves are parties. This use of the independent commission is represented by the following agencies: the Interstate Commerce Commission, the Federal Communications Commission, the Securities and Exchange Commission, the Federal Power Commission, the Federal Trade Commission, the National Bituminous Coal Commission, and the United States Maritime Commission.

For the most part Congress has sought to entrust these commissions with judicial power only to the extent of giving their determination of facts substantial finality in the courts. Thus a common type of statutory provision is the following which relates to the Securities and Exchange Commission and provides that "its finding as to the facts, if supported by substantial evidence, shall be conclusive." [4] But the courts have not only generally recognized the finality of commission determination of facts; in varying though considerable degree they have also recognized a measure of finality in commission determinations of law. [5] The important policy formulating powers of these commissions will be indicated by some references to the broad discretion entrusted to them.

The widest range of policy formulating powers is enjoyed by the Interstate Commerce Commission in its control of the rates, practices, business organization, and financial policy of interstate

---

[4] U. S. Code (1934), Title 15, sec. 78(y).

[5] For the varying though important degree of finality that has been accorded the decisions of the commissions which have existed for some time, see John Dickinson, *Administrative Justice and the Supremacy of the Law*, Ch. III.

railroad and motor carriers. In the matter of rates and practices the commission is empowered to determine what rate or practice "is or will be unjust or unreasonable or unjustly discriminatory or unduly preferential or prejudicial" and to prescribe what will be "just and reasonable."[6] In the matter of business organization, the commission has been empowered to relieve carriers from the operation of the anti-trust laws and to permit combinations or consolidations among them if it determines that such action "will be in the interest of better service to the public, or economy of operation, and will not unduly restrain competition."[7] Finally, with respect to the financial operations of carriers, the commission is empowered to authorize the issuance of capital stock or the assumption of other financial encumbrances when it determines that such action "(a) is for some lawful object within its [carrier's] corporate purposes, and compatible with the public interest . . . is necessary or appropriate for or consistent with the proper performance by the carrier of service to the public . . . and (b) is reasonably necessary and appropriate for such purpose."[8] Substantially the same broad discretionary powers have also been entrusted to the commission in its regulation of interstate motor carrier enterprises.

That these powers involve such broad discretion that their exercise will seriously affect, if not define, the essential character and direction of the nation's policy toward these important economic enterprises, must be conceded. In vesting the commission with these powers Congress has, it is true, provided certain guides or limitations such as, "just and reasonable," "compatible with the public interest," or "reasonably necessary or appropriate." But such vague terms obviously constitute no more than purely formal limitations upon the commission's powers of decision. The other commissions within this group have not been given the same ex-

---

[6] U. S. Code (1934), Title 49, sec. 15(1).
[7] *Ibid.*, sec. 5.   [8] *Ibid.*, sec. 20(2) 2.

tensive range of powers. But such powers as have been given to them similarly involve a significant control over public policy.

Thus, in the government's regulation of interstate wire communicating agencies, Congress has authorized the Federal Communications Commission to determine what are "just and reasonable" rates and business practices [9] and what "public convenience, interest, or necessity requires" in the matter of services.[10] Equally important discretionary powers have also been entrusted to it in connection with radio broadcasting companies. "If public convenience, interest or necessity will be served thereby" the commission is empowered to license such companies to operate,[11] while with respect to their services it is empowered to determine what "public convenience, interest or necessity requires." [12]

In the regulation of national securities exchanges the Securities and Exchange Commission has been empowered to determine what prohibitions, in addition to those specified by Congress, are "necessary and appropriate for the protection of investors or to insure fair dealing in securities." [13] Under the same standard it has also been empowered to suspend for a specified period, or to withdraw entirely, the registration of national securities exchanges,[14] and, subject to the approval of the president, to suspend "summarily" all trading on any national securities exchange for a period not exceeding ninety days.[15]

The Federal Power Commission has been entrusted with broad discretionary powers of control over the development and use of the navigable waters of the United States for water power projects, reservoirs, etc., and over the interstate operations of electric utility companies which are utilizing the navigable waters of the United States for the generation of power. In connection with the development and use of the navigable waters of the United States,

---

[9] *Ibid.*, Title 47, sec. 201(b).   [10] *Ibid.*, sec. 201(a).
[11] *Ibid.*, sec. 307.   [12] *Ibid.*, sec. 303(b).
[13] *Ibid.*, Title 15, sec. 78s(b).   [14] *Ibid.*, sec. 78s(a).   [15] *Ibid.*

the commission has been empowered to decide, in the exercise of its licensing power, when proposed projects "will be best adapted to a comprehensive plan for improving or developing a waterway or waterways for the use or benefit of interstate or foreign commerce, for the improvement and utilization of water power development and for other beneficial public uses." [16] In connection with the interstate operations of electric utility companies it has been authorized to determine what rates are "just and reasonable" [17] and what service is "proper, adequate, or sufficient." [18]

With respect to the conduct of interstate business in general,[19] the Federal Trade Commission has been given power to decide what constitutes "unfair methods of competition" [20] and to prevent the use of such practices if not "in the public interest." [21]

The National Bituminous Coal Commission enjoys broad discretion especially in the formulation of an operator's code for the soft coal industry when operating in or affecting interstate commerce. Thus, in the formulation of the code, the commission is empowered to set the maximum prices for coal; and the law merely provides that the decision to establish maximum prices be made "in the public interest," that the maximum prices be established "at a uniform increase above the minimum prices in effect within the district; so that in the aggregate the maximum prices shall yield a reasonable return above the weighted average cost of the district," and, finally, that no maximum prices be established "for any mine which shall not yield a fair return on the fair value of the property." [22] Industries are not required to accept the code, but, if they refuse, they are subject to a high excise tax.[23]

---

[16] *Ibid.*, Supp. I, Title 16, sec. 803.   [17] *Ibid.*, sec. 824(e).   [18] *Ibid.*

[19] Except those enterprises specifically placed under other authority, such as banks, railroads, etc.

[20] In addition to methods or practices which Congress has itself specifically prohibited.

[21] U. S. Code (1934), Title 15, sec. 45.

[22] *Ibid.*, Supp. III, Title 15, sec. 833(c).   [23] *Ibid.*

Finally, important policy formulating powers have also been entrusted to the United States Maritime Commission. An example is its power to see that "every common carrier by water in interstate commerce shall establish, observe, and enforce just and reasonable rates, fares, charges, classifications, and tariffs, and just and reasonable regulations and practices relating thereto." [24]

A second fairly distinct use being made of the independent commission is represented by the National Labor Relations Board. Like the foregoing commissions this agency has been entrusted with judicial powers in conjunction with administrative powers. It has also been required to proceed for the most part by a process of adjudication and has been empowered to initiate complaints. However, it has been denied any real policy formulating powers. It has been empowered to ensure labor the right to bargain collectively and to prevent unfair labor practices by employers. But Congress has specifically provided what shall constitute collective bargaining and merely empowered the board to determine whether the appropriate unit for the purpose shall be "the employer unit, the craft unit, the plant unit, or subdivision thereof." [25] Similarly, Congress has listed in rather definite terms the labor practices that shall be regarded as "unfair." The following practices are listed: (1) interference with, restraint or coercion of employees in the exercise of their right to self-organization, to form, join, or assist labor organizations, to bargain collectively through representatives of their own choosing, and to engage in concerted activities, for the purpose of collective bargaining or other mutual aid or protection; [26] (2) domination or interference with the formation or administration of any labor organization or contribution of financial or other support to it, provided the employer is not prohibited by the board from per-

---

[24] *Ibid.*, Supp. II, Title 46, sec. 1114.
[25] *Ibid.*, Supp. III, Title 29, sec. 159.
[26] *Ibid.*, secs. 157 and 158.

mitting employees to confer with him during working hours without loss of time or pay; [27] (3) discrimination in regard to hire or tenure of employment or any term or condition of employment in order to encourage or discourage membership in any labor organization, provided that the employer is not precluded from making an agreement with a labor organization to require as a condition of employment membership therein if such labor organization is the representative of the employees under the act; [28] (4) the discharge of an employee or other discrimination against him because he has filed charges or given testimony against the employer; [29] (5) refusal to bargain collectively with the representatives of employees as provided under the act.[30]

A third somewhat different use being made of the independent commission is represented by the Board of Governors of the Federal Reserve System. This agency is being used mainly for the exercise of policy formulating and administrative powers, and in the exercise of these powers it is not required to proceed by a process of adjudication. Only a few judicial powers have been entrusted to the board, although it is required to proceed by a process of adjudication when exercising these judicial powers.[31] With this minor exception, however, the board differs both in powers and procedure from the commissions thus far considered. The policy formulating powers of the board are best indicated by reference to the broad discretion that it enjoys in respect to the volume and distribution of credit throughout the country, the fiscal policy of both the reserve and member banks, and security transactions on national securities exchanges.

In the exercise of its control over the volume and distribution of credit the board is empowered "to supervise and regulate the retirements of Federal Reserve notes and to prescribe rules and

---

[27] *Ibid.*, sec. 158.   [28] *Ibid.*   [29] *Ibid.*   [30] *Ibid.*
[31] *Ibid.*, Title 15, secs. 19, 19(a), 21.

regulations under which such notes may be delivered by the Comptroller of the Currency to the Federal Reserve agents applying therefor," [32] and, further, "to permit or . . . to require the Federal Reserve banks to rediscount the discounted paper of other Federal Reserve banks at rates of interest to be fixed by the Federal Reserve Board [Board of Governors]." [33] Further, the board, or its members, who constitute a majority of the Federal Open Market Committee,[34] has control over the open market operations of all Federal Reserve banks, and control over these operations involves a very significant control over national credit. In vesting the committee with this control the law provides that "no Federal Reserve bank shall engage or decline to engage in open market operations except in accordance with the direction and regulations of the committee," [35] and merely requires that such regulations shall be made "with a view to accommodating commerce and business and with regard to their bearing upon the general credit situation of the country." [36]

In connection with the fiscal policy of member banks of the Federal Reserve System, the board is empowered to fix from time to time for each district and to change upon ten days notice the percentage of their capital and surplus which may be represented by loans secured by stock or bond collateral.[37] Aside from the requirement that no such loans shall exceed ten per cent of the banks' unimpaired capital and surplus, which obviously leaves the board with considerable discretion, the only limitation on the power of the board is that it "establish such percentages with a view to preventing the undue use of bank loans for the speculative carrying of securities." [38]

---

[32] *Ibid.*, Title 12, sec. 248(d).   [33] *Ibid.*, sec. 248(b).

[34] The committee is composed of all seven members of the Board of Governors and five representatives of the Federal Reserve banks, and it operates by majority vote.

[35] U. S. Code (1934), Title 12, sec. 263(b).   [36] *Ibid.*, sec. 263(c).

[37] *Ibid.*, sec. 248(m).   [38] *Ibid.*

For the board's exercise of control over security transactions, Congress has established a schedule of marginal requirements,[39] but it has authorized the board to "(1) prescribe such lower margin requirements for the initial extension or maintenance of credit as it deems necessary or appropriate for the accommodation of commerce and industry, having due regard to the general credit situation of the country, and (2) prescribe such higher margin requirements for the initial extension or maintenance of credit as it deems necessary or appropriate to prevent the excessive use of credit to finance transactions in securities." [40]

A fourth distinct use of the independent commission is represented by the Employees Compensation Commission. This agency has jurisdiction over compensation to employees of the United States for injuries received in service and over compensation to private maritime employees for injuries received in service. Certain related activities are also entrusted to the commission, but in no case is much discretion entrusted to it. Congress has even provided a detailed schedule which the commission must observe in computing compensation rates. The commission is confined to the exercise of administrative and judicial powers. However, its judicial powers are not exercised in conjunction with its administrative powers, and in this it differs from any of the commissions thus far considered. In its exercise of administrative powers the commission is responsible among other things for supervising medical service and physical examinations. In its exercise of judicial powers it is responsible for making compensation awards and it has no responsibility for initiating action or complaints leading to its exercise of judicial powers. Action must be initiated by individuals. It is true that the very nature of its judicial power makes this procedure desirable. But it, nevertheless, constitutes an important difference between this and the other commissions.

---

[39] *Ibid.*, Title 15, sec. 78(g).   [40] *Ibid.*

A fifth distinct use of the independent commission is represented by the Social Security Board which is entrusted with administrative powers only. This agency has been created for the administration of grants-in-aid to the states for old-age assistance, unemployment compensation, aid to the blind, and for the administration of a federal old-age benefit system. The broadest discretion that the board enjoys lies in its power to approve state plans for assistance or compensation. But even here the board's discretion has been very closely confined. A typical example is its discretion in respect to state old-age assistance plans which must be approved by the board as a condition of federal assistance. Any state plan shall be approved, according to the law, when: [41]

1. It provides that it shall be in effect in all political subdivisions of the state, and, if administered by them, be mandatory upon them.

2. It provides for financial participation by the state.

3. It provides for the establishment or designation of a single state agency to administer the plan or supervise administration.

4. It provides for granting to any individual, whose claim for old-age assistance is denied, an opportunity for a fair hearing before such state agency.

5. It provides such methods of administration (other than those relating to selection, tenure of office, and compensation of personnel) as are found by the board to be necessary for the efficient operation of the plan.

6. It provides that the state agency will make such reports, in such form and containing such information, as the board may from time to time require, and comply with such provisions as the board may from time to time find necessary to assure the correctness and verification of such reports.

7. It provides that, if the state or any of its political subdivisions

---

[41] *Ibid.*, Supp. III, Title 42, sec. 302.

collects from the estate of any recipient of old-age assistance any amount with respect to old-age assistance furnished him under the plan, one half of the net amount so collected shall be promptly paid to the United States.

On the other hand, the board is prohibited from approving any state plan which imposes as a condition of eligibility any of the following conditions: (1) an age requirement of more than sixty-five years, except that the plan may impose, effective until January 1, 1940, an age requirement of as much as seventy years; (2) any residence requirement which excludes any resident of the state who has resided therein five years during the nine years immediately preceding the application for old-age assistance and has resided therein continuously for one year immediately preceding the application; (3) any citizenship requirement which excludes any citizen of the United States.

With the Social Security Board should also be included the United States Tariff Commission and the National Mediation Board, since these commissions are also being used simply for the exercise of administrative powers, namely, investigation and mediation.[42] However, because of frequent assertions that these agencies should be excepted from the principles of organization deemed to apply to the exercise of administrative powers in general, separate consideration will be accorded them in the discussion of organization.

---

[42] Objection may be made to this classification of the Tariff Commission as an organ of investigation only, because of its power to determine "unfair practices" in import trade. However, such determination becomes effective only if acted upon by the president. See U. S. Code (1934), Title 19, sec. 1337.

CHAPTER TWO

The Status of the Independent Commission

THOUGH NONE of these commissions have been made subject in law to presidential direction, there are, at present, various factors which enable the president to exert a very strong influence upon their action. The first, and most important, is the uncertainty of tenure that still exists. For the members of these agencies do not yet enjoy definite legal security against the president's arbitrary exercise of the removal power, and until they enjoy that security they are hardly in a position to ignore entirely presidential wishes. This removal power, moreover, has been the principal means by which the president has elevated himself to the commanding position that he now enjoys over the federal administrative organization. Further, it has not been generally necessary for the president to actually use this power to secure obedience to his wishes. The more possession of the power, as a constant and implied threat of punitive action if presidential wishes are not obeyed, has usually sufficed.

Complete independence of action and insecurity of tenure are not incompatible, if a tradition of presidential noninterference has developed. But no such tradition has yet developed in the president's relationships with these commissions. Even in the act of setting up the Federal Reserve Board, which marked the real beginning of the trend toward the use of commissions, the first act of the president was to nominate for membership only men of his own party who had also apparently voted the party ticket.[1]

For a long time a tradition of noninterference in the president's relations with the Interstate Commerce Commission appeared to be a definite development. But that tradition was apparently not well enough developed to deter President Harding from attempting to influence the commission's action. Professor Sharfman observes that:

> During the Harding administration when the commission was struggling with the problem of rate adjustments, there were unmistakable evidences of attempted executive influence. Relief to agriculture, as one aspect of special rate treatment to "basic" commodities, was accepted as an administration policy, and its adoption appears to have been urged upon the commission and some of its individual members even by the President himself.[2]

President Harding also apparently sought to influence the action of the United States Tariff Commission. In fact, it was testified that he sought to "make over the Commission" itself by a variety of expedients, such as offers of other federal posts to existing members and requests for undated letters of resignation before appointing new members.[3]

President Coolidge followed the example of his predecessors and in one instance, at least, appeared to be particularly successful in influencing the action of one of these commissions. That instance occurred in 1925 when he appointed William E. Humphrey to the Federal Trade Commission and thus swung the balance of power in the commission over to its Republican membership. The effect of that appointment, according to *Nation's Business*, was particularly manifest in a "narrowed conception of the Commission's functions and a broad tolerance of business

---

[1] *Cong. Rec.*, 63rd Cong., 2nd sess., p. 12648.

[2] Isaiah L. Sharfman, *The Interstate Commerce Commission*, II, 455.

[3] Cited *ibid.*, pp. 455–59.

behavior," [4] policies too well identified with the Coolidge administration to require any comment. President Coolidge, however, left little doubt of his intention to affect the action of the commission or, in fact, of his conception that it, as well as other commissions, was properly subordinate to the will of the president. According to Senator Carter Glass:

When Mr. Humphrey was appointed a member of the Federal Trade Commission it was announced if not by the White House spokesman, with quite as much apparent authority as that gentleman appeared to assume, that he was put on the commission to halt its inquisitiveness, to change the order of its activities and to revolutionize by restraining its methods of procedure. The statement was even made that it was the conviction of the President that this and other commissions should subordinate their judgments to the opinions of the executive, and that they were mere agencies to register the policies of the administration. [5]

President Hoover, also, attempted to influence the action of these commissions. [6] But under the present Roosevelt administration a far more aggressive attitude has been taken than by any of the preceding presidents: the president has actually resorted to the use of the removal power. In the early part of his administration, President Roosevelt secured the resignation of Dr. George O. Smith of the Federal Power Commission and removed William E. Humphrey of the Federal Trade Commission. Mr. Humphrey had refused to resign, and in the correspondence that ensued the president frankly admitted that he objected to Mr.

---

[4] July, 1927, p. 30, cited *ibid.*, p. 459, note 209. See also in this connection Thomas C. Blaisdell, *The Federal Trade Commission*, p. 82.

[5] *Cong. Rec.*, 70th Cong., 1st sess., p. 3031, cited in Sharfman, *The Interstate Commerce Commission*, II, 459, note 209. For attempts by President Coolidge to influence other commissions, see James Hart, *Tenure of Office under the Constitution*, pp. 156–70.   [6] See Sharfman, II, 456–58.

Humphrey solely because of the latter's conception of Federal Trade Commission policy.[7]

Mr. Humphrey, shortly thereafter, brought action in the Court of Claims to recover the salary allegedly due him. The case finally went to the Supreme Court of the United States, which held the removal to be illegal.[8] This was the first decision actually involving the tenure of any of these commissioners, but its full significance can only be understood after an examination of the theory of the president's removal power which the courts had developed up to the time of the decision.[9]

Prior to this decision it had become rather clearly settled that, regardless of any statutory grant, the president possessed the power to remove all administrative officers who, like these commissioners, were appointed by the president with the consent of the Senate. This inherent power of removal was held by the court to be incident to the power of appointment, whether conferred by Congress or the Constitution, and the real act of appointment was regarded for judicial purposes as being performed by the president alone.

Thus, in referring to a statutory provision, though not the one involved in the case, which provided that district attorneys who were appointed by the president and Senate could be removed "at pleasure," the court declared:

The provision for removal from office at pleasure was not necessary for the exercise of that power by the President because of the fact that he was then regarded as being clothed with that power in any event . . . and we think the provision that the officials were removable from office at pleasure was but a recognition of the construction thus

---

[7] *The Sun* (Baltimore), Nov. 12, 1933.

[8] *Rathbun* v. *U. S.*, 295 U. S. 602 (1934).

[9] The question of the president's removal power has rested entirely with the courts because no mention is made of that power in the Constitution.

almost universally adhered to and acquiesced in as to the power of the President to remove.[10]

Similarly, in a later case the court said:

The right of removal would exist if the statute had not contained a word upon the subject. It does not exist by virtue of the grant, but it inheres in the right to appoint, unless limited by Constitution or statute.[11]

Whether the president's power to remove any of these officers was illimitable, or subject to limitation by Congress, had not been actually decided until 1926 in the case of *Myers* v. *U. S.* But, before this decision, there seemed reason to believe that the president's power was illimitable in respect to some officers and limitable in respect to others.

In *U. S.* v. *Germaine* the court had roughly classified administrative officers in the following passage:

The Constitution for purposes of appointment very clearly divides all its officers into two classes. The primary class requires a nomination by the President and a confirmation by the Senate. But, foreseeing that when officers became numerous and sudden removals necessary, this mode might be inconvenient, it was provided that, in regard to officers inferior to those specifically mentioned, Congress might by law vest their appointment in the President alone, in the courts of law, or in the heads of departments.[12]

For convenience the first class will be referred to as "superior" officers and the second class as "inferior" officers. This classification with the heads of the departments clearly in the first class served to guide the court, and, prior to the Myers case, the law seemed to be that Congress could not restrict the president's power

---

[10] *Parsons* v. *U. S.*, 167 U. S. 324, 339 (1897).

[11] *Shurtleff* v. *U. S.*, 189 U. S. 311, 316 (1902). See also *Ex parte Hennen*, 13 Pet. 230, 258 (1839).

[12] 99 U. S. 482, 483 (1879).

to remove superior officers appointed by him and the Senate, but that it could restrict his power to remove inferior officers.

In no case had the court actually held that Congress could not restrict the president's power to remove superior officers. But the so-called Legislative Decision of 1789, in which the very first Congress apparently conceded the president's constitutional and hence illimitable power to remove such officers,[13] had been generally accepted in practice;[14] and the court had at least expressed some doubt respecting the right of Congress to restrict presidential removal of these officers. In *U. S.* v. *Perkins* the court cited and approved the following passage from a decision by the Court of Claims: "Whether or not Congress can restrict the power of removal incident to the power of appointment of those officers who are appointed by the President by and with the advice and consent of the Congress under the authority of the Constitution (article 2 sec. 2) does not arise in this case and need not be decided."[15]

On the other hand, the court had left little doubt that Congress could restrict the president's power to remove inferior officers even though appointed by him and the Senate. This was definitely implied in the following passage of the Shurtleff case: "To take away this power of removal in relation to an inferior officer created by statute, although that statute provided for an appointment thereto by the President and confirmation by the Senate, would require very clear and explicit language."[16] Furthermore, the intention of Congress in this case was made the turning point of the decision, although the court gave a

---

[13] See Frank J. Goodnow, *Principles of the Administrative Law of the United States*, pp. 76–77.

[14] With the exception of the Tenure-of-Office Acts which Congress later repealed.

[15] 116 U. S. 483 (1885).

[16] *Shurtleff* v. *U. S.*, 189 U. S. 311, 315 (1902). See also *Ex parte Hennen*, 13 Pet. 230, 258 (1839), *U. S.* v. *Perkins*, 116 U. S. 483 (1885).

strange interpretation to the intention of Congress in holding that a provision which specified causes for removal did not limit the president to removal for those causes only.

In the case of *Myers* v. *U. S.*, which followed the Shurtleff case, the court, however, took a much more aggressive stand, and, while its decision did not directly involve members of these commissions, it did raise serious doubts concerning their right to independence. This case concerned a first class postmaster and a statutory provision stating that such officers "shall be appointed and may be removed by the President by and with the advice and consent of the Senate." President Wilson removed Myers, a postmaster of this class, before the expiration of his term and without the advice and consent of the Senate. The officer involved was clearly within the category of "inferior" officers according to the Germaine case, and the intention of Congress to restrict the president's power to remove him was plain. The court, however, disregarded the implications of previous decisions and held that all executive officers, "superior" or "inferior," were subject to the president's illimitable power of removal so long as their appointment had been entrusted by the Constitution or statute to the president and the Senate.[17]

The opinion of the court was founded essentially on its interpretation of the Legislative Decision of 1789 as an exposition of the Constitution to this effect by the first Congress and upon its own interpretation of the Constitution which it derived from two broad premises.

On the one hand, the court held, in accordance with past decisions, that the power of removal inhered in the power to appoint and that despite the Senate's share in the appointment the president alone was to be regarded as actually performing that function. On the other hand, and principally, the court held that Article II of the Constitution was a grant to the president of

[17] 272 U. S. 52 (1926).

plenary executive power. In so holding, it made no distinction between powers specifically conferred upon the president by the Constitution and those which owed their existence to statute alone; once created they became presidential powers.

To substantiate this intention of Article II, the court cited the faithful execution clause of the Constitution as commanding the president to supervise the performance of all executive duties once created.

From this broad interpretation of Article II, it deduced as necessary to that supervision the president's illimitable power to remove all executive officers, when appointed by the president and Senate. Obviously, this interpretation of Article II was broad enough to permit a deduction of the president's illimitable power to remove all executive officers, however appointed, and flexible enough to include or exclude, as the court might see fit, any number of offices that Congress might create. For with the rejection of the theory that executive power was defined in the constitutional enumeration, there remained no objective restraint to any expansion of the term which the court might think desirable.

The majority of commentators were disposed to except the members of these commissions from the application of this case. They relied principally upon the ordinary significance of the term "executive" and upon the fact that the officer involved in the Myers case, a first class postmaster, was only entrusted with the ordinary duties of presidential subordinates, while these commissioners, or most of them, are entrusted with extraordinary or exceptional tasks.

Mr. James Beck, who argued the Myers case in support of the president's power, best expressed this view when he said:

Moreover the [Myers] decision does not decide whether or not there may not be a class of officers who are not in strictness executive officers. For example, the Federal Trade Commission is chiefly a fact-finding commission to aid Congress in formulating legislation.

The Interstate Commerce Commission is a fact-finding commission which discharges the so-called legislative duty of imposing reasonable rates upon carriers. . . . Can the President remove such quasi-legislative officers? This decision is not conclusive upon this point, and properly so; for no case of this character was before the Court.[18]

On the other hand, a few commentators had contended that the decision definitely brought the members of these commissions under the president's illimitable power of removal,[19] and it must be conceded that the court itself appeared to regard these officers as sufficiently "executive" in character to be subject to this power. With specific reference to officers of this type the court said:

Of course there may be duties so peculiarly and specifically entrusted to the discretion of a particular officer as to raise the question whether the President may over-rule and revise the officer's interpretation of his statutory duty. Then there may be duties of a quasi-judicial character imposed on executive officers and members of executive tribunals whose decisions after notice and hearing affect the interests of individuals, the discharge of which the President cannot in a particular case properly influence or control. But even in such case he may consider the decision after its rendition as a reason for removing the officer on the ground that the discretion entrusted to that officer has not been intelligently or wisely exercised. Otherwise he does not discharge his duties of seeing that the laws be faithfully executed.[20]

---

[18] *New York Times*, Nov. 7, 1926, quoted in Westel W. Willoughby, *Constitutional Law*, III, sec. 1000. See also William F. Willoughby, *Legal Status and Functions of the General Accounting Office of the National Government*, pp. 12–15; Westel W. Willoughby, *Constitutional Law*, III, secs. 1525–27; John M. Mathews, *American Constitutional System*, p. 165.

[19] See Charles E. Morganston, *The Appointing and Removal Power of the President of the United States*, pp. 128ff.; Charles A. Beard and William Beard, *The American Leviathan*, pp. 272–73.

[20] 272 U. S. 52, 135 (1926). This faithful execution clause, it is to be noted, was the principal source from which the court purported to derive the president's possession of plenary executive power and hence of an illimitable power of removal.

Again, with specific reference to the members of these commissions, the court said:

Since the provision for an Interstate Commerce Commission in 1887, many administrative boards have been created whose members are appointed by the President by and with the advice and consent of the Senate, and in the statutes creating them have been provisions for the removal of the members for specified causes. Such provisions are claimed to be inconsistent with the independent power of removal by the President. This, however, is shown to be unfounded by the case of Shurtleff v. U. S. . . . That case concerned an act creating a Board of General Appraisers . . . and provided for their removal for inefficiency, neglect of duty, or malfeasance in office. . . . Assuming for the purposes of that case only but without deciding that Congress might limit the President's power to remove, the court held that the President could, by virtue of his general power of appointment, remove an officer though appointed by and with the advice and consent of the Senate and notwithstanding specific statutory provisions for his removal, on the ground that the power of removal inhered in the power to appoint. This is an indication that many of the statutes cited are to be reconciled with the unrestricted power of the President to remove if he chooses to exercise the power.[21]

The recent Rathbun case, however, has definitely eliminated the constitutional doubt raised by the Myers case and has declared that Congress can, in fact, limit the president's power to remove the members of these commissions, so long as they are not confined to purely executive powers. That case concerned the removal of Mr. Humphrey of the Federal Trade Commission, already referred to, in the face of statutory provisions which, in addition to fixing a definite term of years for the members, provide that any member may be removed by the president for "inefficiency, neglect of duty or malfeasance in office." [22]

---

[21] *Ibid.*, 171–72.
[22] U. S. Code (1934), Title 15, sec. 41.

In removing Mr. Humphrey, the president disregarded the causes specified in the statute and justified his action on the ground that Mr. Humphrey was not in sympathy with the president in regard to the policy that the Federal Trade Commission ought to pursue. "You will, I know," said the president, "realize that I do not feel that your mind and my mind go along together on either the policies or the administering of the Federal Trade Commission, and, frankly, I think it is best for the people of this country that I should have full confidence." [23]

Deciding against the validity of the removal the court undertook to answer two questions which had been certified to it by the Court of Claims—namely, (1) Do the provisions . . . restrict or limit the power of the president to remove a commissioner except upon one or more of the causes named? (2) If so, is such restriction or limitation valid under the Constitution of the United States?

In answering the second question in the affirmative, the court relied principally upon the character of the tasks entrusted to the commission. Such tasks, it held, were not purely "executive," as those of the officer involved in the Myers case, but were primarily quasi-legislative and quasi-judicial. The opinion of the court reads:

The office of a postmaster is so essentially unlike the office now involved that the decision in the Myers case cannot be accepted as controlling our decision here. A postmaster is an executive officer restricted to the performance of executive functions. He is charged with no duty at all related to either the legislative or judicial power. The actual decision in the Myers case finds support in the theory that such an officer is merely one of the units in the executive department and, hence, inherently subject to the exclusive and illimitable power of removal by the chief executive whose subordinate and aid he is. Putting aside dicta . . . the necessary reach of the Myers decision

---

[23] *The Sun*, (Baltimore), Nov. 12, 1933.

goes far enough to include all purely executive officers. It goes no farther; much less does it include an officer who occupies no place in the executive department and who exercises no part of the executive power vested by the Constitution in the President. The Federal Trade Commission is an administrative body created by Congress to carry into effect legislative policies . . . and to perform other specified duties as a legislative and judicial aid. . . . We think it plain under the Constitution that illimitable power of removal is not possessed by the President in respect of offices of the character of those just named. The authority of Congress, in creating quasi-legislative or quasi-judicial agencies, to require them to act in the discharge of their duties independent of executive control cannot well be doubted. . . .[24]

The constitutional question concerning three of these commissions which, according to this study are confined to administrative powers,[25] was not in issue before the court; and in fact these three commissions would seem to be subject to the president's constitutional removal power under the decision in the Myers case. However, the court in the Rathbun case raised some doubt on this question; for it apparently recognized a class of powers in between purely executive powers, on the one hand, and quasi-legislative and quasi-judicial powers, on the other hand; and it left the constitutional question open in respect to officers or agencies exercising such powers. Thus the court said in the following passage:

To the extent that, between the decision in the Myers case, which sustains the unrestricted power of the President to remove purely executive officers, and our present decision that such power does not extend to an officer such as that here involved, there shall remain a field of doubt, we leave such cases as may fall within it for future consideration and determination as they may arise.[26]

---

[24] 295 U. S. 602 (1934).

[25] Namely, the Social Security Board, the United States Tariff Commission, and the National Mediation Board.

[26] 295 U. S. 602, 632 (1934).

In effect, therefore, the court, in apparently recognizing this un-defined class of powers, created some uncertainty as to whether the powers of these three commissions would be classified in a future case as purely executive or as something else and hence left uncertain the constitutional removal power of the president in respect to these three commissions.[27]

With the exception, however, of the three commissions men-tioned, the plain effect of the Rathbun decisions was to make the problem of securing the members of these commissions against the president's removal power primarily a legislative problem. But, until other action is taken, the members by no means enjoy certain protection against the president's arbitrary exercise of the removal power. The restrictive effect of certain statutory pro-visions common to a number of these commissions was, of course, in issue before the court. But the court did not adequately enough show the restrictive effect of these provisions, while two other distinct types of provisions are to be found in connection with some of these commissions. In the examination of the statutory provisions which follows, the Social Security Board, the United States Tariff Commission, and the National Mediation Board will be included with the understanding, however, that Congress may not have the constitutional power to restrict the president's power to remove their members.

The statutory provisions involved in the Rathbun case itself stated that "the first commissioners appointed shall continue in office for terms of three, four, five, six and seven years respec-tively . . . but their successors shall be appointed for terms of seven years. . . . Any commissioner may be removed by the president for inefficiency, neglect of duty, or malfeasance in of-fice." The court held that these provisions manifested a suf-ficient intention on the part of Congress to restrict the president

---

[27] It is recognized that the court may classify differently from the author the powers of some of the other commissions.

to removals for the specific causes named. In establishing this intention of Congress, the court did not rely solely upon the statutory provisions. It cited the legislative reports and debates to show the intention of Congress to establish an independent unit and the quasi-legislative and quasi-judicial tasks of the commission to show the necessity for its independent position. But, at least, it placed equal reliance upon the statutory provisions themselves.

In concluding that these provisions showed an intention to restrict the president's removal power, it relied upon the use of the words "continue in office," the establishment of definite terms for the members, and the provision specifying that the president might remove a member for certain causes. The language of the court in this connection is as follows:

The government says the phrase "continue in office" is of no legal significance and, moreover, applies to the first commissioners. We think it has significance. It may be that, literally, its application is restricted as suggested but it, nevertheless, lends support to a view contrary to that of the government as to the meaning of the entire requirement in respect of tenure for it is not easy to suppose that Congress intended to secure the first commissioners against removal for the causes specified and deny like security to their successors.[28]

Putting this phrase aside, however, the fixing of a definite term subject to removal for cause is enough to establish the legislative intent that the term is not to be curtailed in the absence of such cause.

The principal doubt that still remains in connection with this type of statutory provision concerns the actual effect that will be given to the restriction which they seek to impose upon the president's power. In addition to the Federal Trade Commission,

---

[28] It is much easier to suppose that Congress attached no significance to the phrase. Otherwise it would hardly have omitted to use it in both connections and, in any event, it would certainly have been more careful to use it in the second than in the first connection.

the commissions for which this type of provision or others of similar import have been established are: the Interstate Commerce Commission,[29] the National Bituminous Coal Commission,[30] the National Labor Relations Board,[31] the United States Maritime Commission,[32] and the National Mediation Board.[33]

The plain purpose sought in the restriction is to confine the president's removal power to instances where clear dereliction of duty exists and thus to exclude his use of that power as a coercive instrument. But no intimation was given by the court as to how that purpose was to be effectively safeguarded. The court's declaration that the president could remove a commissioner only for the specific causes named is probably also to be read in conjunction with the dictum in both *Reagan* v. *U. S.*[34] and *Shurtleff* v. *U. S.*[35] This dictum was to the effect that the president must accord notice and hearing to an officer before removing him for causes prescribed by statute. But the requirement of notice and hearing will not suffice in itself to protect adequately the members of these commissions against the president's coercive use of the removal power. They will be adequately protected only if the court will undertake to determine upon complaint the actual sufficiency of causes for removal, and there is some question whether the court will do this. It is quite likely that it will hold that the terms inefficiency, neglect of duty, and malfeasance in office are sufficiently vague to presuppose a considerable exercise

---

[29] U. S. Code (1934), Title 49, sec. 11.

[30] *Ibid.*, Supp. III, Title 15, sec. 829.

[31] *Ibid.*, Supp. I, Title 29, sec. 153.

[32] 49 Stat. L. 1985, sec. 201(a).

[33] U. S. Code (1934), Title 45, sec. 154. The third and fifth have an added provision that removal shall be "for no other cause." But in view of the Rathbun decision such additional words can have no additional significance. The words "continue in office" are omitted in the provisions concerning most of these agencies. But this is hardly significant enough to except such agencies from the law of the Rathbun case.

[34] 182 U. S. 419, 425 (1900).   [35] 189 U. S. 311, 317 (1902).

of discretion by the president and that, in accordance with its general attitude toward discretionary acts, it will accord him considerable, if not complete, finality in their determination.

Such finality has been generally accorded in the states where statutory provisions similar to these have been involved.[86] At least two decisions have held that even notice and hearing is unnecessary,[87] but almost uniformly the contrary position has been taken.[88] In only two states, however, does it appear that the courts have asserted the right to review the actual sufficiency of causes for removal.[89] Whether the general tendency among state courts will have any weight with the federal judiciary remains to be seen; but, in any event, the essential fact with regard to the commissions having this type of statutory provision is that the actual security of their members against the president's coercive use of the removal power still remains in doubt. Public opinion or a sense of duty might, in fact, restrain the president in his use of the removal power, but the operation of these forces would be too uncertain to give the members a very strong feeling of security.

In addition to the type of statutory provisions just discussed, two other distinct types are to be found in connection with some of these commissions. One of them is found only in connection with the Board of Governors of the Federal Reserve System.

---

[86] *Wilcox* v. *People*, 90 Ill. 186 (1878); *State* v. *Henry*, 60 Fla. 246 (1910); *State* v. *Wilson*, 121 N. C. 425 (1897); *State* v. *Hay*, 45 Neb. 321 (1895); *State* v. *Frazier*, 48 Ga. 137 (1873).

[87] *Wilcox* v. *People*, 90 Ill. 186 (1878); *People ex rel. Fonda* v. *Morton*, 148 N. Y. 156 (1896).

[88] *Dullam* v. *Wilson*, 53 Mich. 392 (1884); *Biggs* v. *McBride*, 17 Ore. 640 (1889); *In re Guden*, 171 N. Y. 529 (1902); *Ham* v. *Boston Police Board*, 142 Mass. 90 (1886); *State* v. *Hawkins*, 44 Ohio St. 98 (1886); *State ex rel. Denison* v. *St. Louis*, 90 Mo. 19 (1886).

[89] New York and Ohio. See *Masterson* v. *French*, 110 N. Y. 494 (1888); *People* v. *Wright*, 7 App. Div. (N. Y.) 185 (1896); *State ex rel. Meader* v. *Sullivan*, 58 Ohio St. 504 (1892).

This type fixes definite terms for the members of the board but provides that any member may be removed by the president "for cause." [40] It obviously accords the members even less security against the president's use of the removal power. It specifically grants the president the right to determine what are causes for removal, and, though he may be required to observe notice and hearing procedure, there is little to justify interference by the courts with his determination of sufficient causes regardless of their character.

The other and final distinct type of statutory provisions raises more doubtful questions. This type merely provides definite terms of years, although for three of these commissions the words "continue in office" have been used as in the provisions involved in the Rathbun case. It does not specify any causes for removal and, in fact, it makes no mention of the removal power. The commissions with this type of provision are the following: The Federal Communications Commission,[41] the Securities and Exchange Commission,[42] the Federal Power Commission,[43] the Employees Compensation Commission,[44] the U. S. Tariff Commission,[45] and the Social Security Board.[46]

The security of the members of these commissions against the president's arbitrary exercise of the removal power remains in doubt only if it be assumed that the president's inherent removal power extends to them as well as to "executive" officers. This question was not answered by the court in the Rathbun case; the statute before the court specifically provided for the president's exercise of the removal power. But the language in the decision seemed to imply that such power was conceded. Thus the court stated the essential question before it to be "whether the power of

---

[40] U. S. Code (1934), Supp. I, Title 12, sec. 242.

[41] *Ibid.*, Title 47, sec. 154(c).   [42] *Ibid.*, Title 15, sec. 78(d).

[43] *Ibid.*, Title 16, sec. 792.   [44] *Ibid.*, Title 5, seç. 778.

[45] *Ibid.*, Title 19, sec. 1330(b).   [46] *Ibid.*, Supp. III, Title 42, sec. 901.

the President to remove an officer shall prevail over the authority
of Congress to condition the power . . ." and this apparent con-
cession, it will be noted, was in direct line with the theory of
the president's inherent removal power as it had been developed
in past decisions. No attempt had been made to limit that power
to where only executive officers were involved. It had been applied equally to where members of the Customs Court, formerly
Board of General Appraisers, were involved.[47]

If it may be assumed, then, that the president's inherent power
of removal extends to these commissioners, two further questions
are presented which will have to be decided before their actual
security against the president's coercive use of the removal power
is established. These questions are: first, can Congress deny outright the president's exercise of this inherent power; [48] and second,
if so, is such a denial sufficiently clear where the statutory provisions omit to mention the removal power and merely specify
a definite term of years, or, in some cases also use the words
"continue in office." [49]

The first question has never been touched upon by the court.
Presumably it will be decided in the affirmative on the theory
that the power to restrict includes the power to deny outright.
But it still remains an open question. The second question will
probably be decided in the affirmative, also, if the court will give
primary consideration to the following: first, its conception of
the need for independence where quasi-legislative and quasi-

---

[47] *Shurtleff* v. *U. S.*, 189 U. S. 311 (1902).

[48] In the Rathbun case the issue before the court was merely one of restricting
the president's exercise of the removal power, since the statute involved provided
for removal by the president.

[49] These words are used in connection with the Federal Communications Commission, the Federal Power Commission, the Federal Trade Commission, and the
United States Tariff Commission. But they are not used in connection with the
Securities and Exchange Commission, the Employees Compensation Commission,
and the Social Security Board.

judicial duties are involved as stated in the Rathbun case, and, second, the fact that a contrary decision would leave the president without any restriction whatsoever in the exercise of the removal power.

On the other hand, it is equally probable that, while the court will acknowledge the importance of these factors, it will take the position that Congress must express in the statutory provisions themselves a clear intention to deny the president the power to remove and that failure to do so justifies the conclusion that no such denial was intended. Should the court take this position, it does not seem likely that it will find a sufficiently clear intention manifested in these provisions, though they do contain certain elements which were held in the Rathbun case to substantiate an intention to restrict the president's power.[50] Thus, all of them specify a definite term of years, while for three of these commissions they also contain the words "continue in office" when referring to the terms of the first commissioners.[51] But these elements were used in the Rathbun case only to buttress the court's conclusion that the provisions as a whole showed an intention to

---

[50] Even if the court should go beyond the statutory provisions and give some recognition to the legislative reports and debates, it will have some difficulty showing a clear intention to establish independent units, except perhaps in the case of the Social Security Board. See *H. R. Rep.* 615, p. 29, 74th Cong., 1st sess. In connection with the Communications Commission and the Securities and Exchange Commission no mention is made of the status sought to be accorded. Some mention is made of the status sought to be accorded the Federal Power Commission and the Employees Compensation Commission, but no clear intention is shown. See in connection with the Federal Power Commission, *Cong. Rec.*, 71st Cong., 2nd sess., pp. 10332–33; in connection with the Employees Compensation Commission, see *H. R. Rep.* 678, p. 12, 64th Cong., 1st sess. On the other hand the only statement that occurs with respect to the United States Tariff Commission, as reorganized in 1930, seems to imply a recognition that the members were subject to the president's unrestricted removal power. See *Cong. Rec.*, 71st Cong., 1st sess., p. 3032.

[51] See note 49.

restrict the president. They were not held to be sufficient in themselves, and it is certainly questionable whether the court will hold them to be so.

Until all of these legal uncertainties in respect to tenure have been resolved in favor of the independent position of these commissions, their power to maintain at all times independence in fact is likely to be considerably impaired. Few of their members can develop a full feeling of independence or the courage to oppose the wishes of the president, unless they feel entirely secure from his coercive use of the removal power. As is evident from the preceding discussion, these legal uncertainties are the result of both congressional and judicial equivocation. But the major cause has been congressional equivocation, and the major responsibility for eliminating these uncertainties, if complete independence is actually desired, rests with Congress.

Another less direct and important source of presidential influence is the method of appointment now provided for all of these commissioners—namely, appointment by the president with the consent of the Senate. This power enables a president to nominate only those men who are in entire sympathy with his program, and, further, serves as a constant threat to members whose term will expire during a president's term that they will not be named for reappointment, unless their decisions conform to the president's wishes. This is especially true in view of the infrequency of reappointments during the life of these commissions. In a recent study, Professor E. Pendleton Herring says:

The Interstate Commerce Commission is really the only commission where the principle of reappointment has been followed by our Presidents with any degree of consistency. Down to the present [1936] 43 men have been appointed to this commission and 26 of these have been reappointed. . . . A review of the other commissions shows how unusual it is for a President to reappoint commissioners. Ten men were reappointed to serve on the Tariff Commission but in only two cases do we find a President of one party reappointing a commissioner of the opposite party when this commissioner was the original appointee of the President of the same opposing party.[52]

Farther on Professor Herring shows that from a total of 143 first appointments up to 1936, there were only 56 second appointments, 17 third appointments, 3 fourth appointments, and 1 fifth appointment.[53]

The above figures also serve to indicate that the president has used his appointing power to further his views of national policy, and this is Professor Herring's conclusion. "In making appointments," he declares, "the President is engaged in an act of policy. His conception of the purpose and function of a particular commission is exemplified in the men he selects to administer the agency." [54]

Congress has, it is true, modified the actual influence which a president might otherwise possess by reason of his appointing power. The terms of the members of these commissions have been staggered with the consequence that a president can seldom appoint during one presidential term a majority of the members of a commission. But the terms are still so short that a very frequent exercise of the appointing power is possible. For, with the exception of the Board of Governors of the Federal Reserve System,[55] the terms are no greater than seven years and in one instance as low as three years.

To reduce or eliminate this influence which the president possesses by reason of his appointing power, there are two steps that might be suggested. The first is to lengthen considerably the terms of office thus reducing the frequency of appointments.

---

[52] *Federal Commissioners—A Study of Their Careers and Qualifications,* p. 81.
[53] *Ibid.,* Appendix P, p. 144.   [54] *Ibid.,* p. 77.
[55] The members of the Board of Governors of the Federal Reserve System have terms of fourteen years. U. S. Code (1934), Supp. I, Title 12, sec. 241.

The second is to transfer the power of appointment to some organ of government less likely to use the power for purposes of influence. However, in view of the broad policy formulating powers of these commissions, it would be difficult to find any organ of government which would not be likely to use the power for purposes of influence. It would apparently be constitutional to entrust this power to the Supreme Court.[56] But it is questionable whether the court itself would use the power with more impartiality than the president in view of the extent to which it has used its theoretically impartial function of judicial review to further its own views respecting national policy. Whether appointment should be entrusted to the Supreme Court or left with the president, it would at least, however, appear desirable to lengthen considerably the terms of office of these commissioners, if the fullest measure of independence is desired.

Another source of presidential influence, or a factor which facilitates presidential influence, is the statutory provision which provides that no more than a majority of the members of any of these commissions shall be of the same political party. This provision is used in connection with all but the Board of Governors of the Federal Reserve System. During the debate which preceded the creation of the Federal Trade Commission, the value of this type of provision was made an issue for the first time. The issue was raised in the Senate and a decision was made in favor of the provision after Senator Nelson pointed out that the absence of such a provision in the case of the Board of Governors of the Federal Reserve System [57] had made it possible for President Wilson to exclude all but Democrats from membership on the board.[58]

Disregarding this violence to party feeling—Senator Nelson

---

[56] Article II, sec. 2, clause 2.
[57] Then called the Federal Reserve Board.
[58] *Cong. Rec.*, 63rd Cong., 2nd sess., p. 12648.

was a Republican—the measure of the president's influence over the board would not have been appreciably lessened if provision had been made for bipartisanship. For all of these commissions except the U. S. Tariff Commission are necessarily provided with an odd number of members and a bipartisan provision would merely have prevented President Wilson from having more than a controlling number of men of his own party on the board.

Aside from purely negative effects, this bipartisan provision has certain results which are clearly destructive of independent action. In the first place, it specifically encourages the maintenance within these commissions of party lines and thus, in keeping alive a feeling of party loyalty, seems to ensure that the president will always have a certain influence over the members of these commissions who belong to his party. In the second place it consistently assures each president that he will have upon assuming office at least a minority of his party on these agencies and that he will in many cases only have to wait until the term of one member expires before having a majority. The existence of this condition of partisanship among the members of the Federal Trade Commission and the opportunity offered the president were both clearly manifest when the appointment by President Coolidge of a single member to the commission was accompanied by a successful reversal of the commission's policy.[59]

A final source of presidential influence is the president's budget power. Requests for appropriations must be approved in the first instance by the president. Even after the appropriations have been voted by Congress, the president may, if he chooses, exercise a certain measure of control over the expenditure of the appropriations. Through his subordinates he is empowered to make monthly allotments of funds based on acceptable work programs, though this power has not been used to any important extent.

This raises a very difficult problem for the proponents of inde-

[59] See above, pp. 17–18.

pendence, because it would not be consistent with good budgetary practice to except the appropriations of these agencies from presidential control.   Provision for central planning of all expenditures is considered essential to effective budgeting.   Whether good budgetary practice should be sacrificed in this case will depend upon the importance attached to independence.   It is sufficient here to point out this very real problem that faces those who favor commission independence.

CHAPTER THREE

Independence and Board Control

IN THIS chapter the desirability of independence and board control will be examined in terms of the powers entrusted to these commissions. Organization is, of course, only one factor in effective government. Another and more important factor is personnel. But however good the personnel, the best results can hardly be obtained unless the principles of organization are those best adapted to the type of work to be performed. Whether independence and board control seem to be best adapted to the types of work assigned to these commissions is the question to be discussed here.

Quite a number of these commissions have been severely criticized in recent days. In arguing against an increase in the appropriations for the National Bituminous Coal Commission, Representative Dirksen declared in the last Congress: "The most charitable thing that can be said of the commission and its operations is that it has made a most inglorious and pitiful record thus far. . . . It seems that the defence of the commission and the desire to augment its appropriations comes from the states which fared best at the patronage trough." [1] Equally severe was the criticism of the commission by its Acting Director of Trial

---

[1] *Cong. Rec.*, 75th Cong., 3rd sess., p. 3372. See also *ibid.*, pp. 3373–74; *Cong. Rec.*, 75th Cong., 2nd sess., pp. 253–55.

Examiners shortly after his resignation.[2] Such criticisms make this discussion of the main features of commission organization particularly timely.

Unfortunately, such a discussion can not draw heavily or with much confidence upon the lessons of experience. For there has been extremely little experience with other principles of organization except where administrative power alone is to be exercised. Even more important, there has been in no case such supervised experimentation as to make possible an intimate comparison of different principles of organization with proper allowance for differences in personnel and for differences in the problems confronting a new agency and its predecessor. But however inconclusive this discussion may be, it is hoped that it will be of some value in suggesting the need for experimentation and in aiding intelligent supervision of such experimentation by pointing out performance features entitled to particular observation.

Where, in addition to their other functions, these commissions have been entrusted with judicial power, there has been a noticeable tendency to justify their independent position in terms of that power alone. Thus, Professor Isaiah L. Sharfman says in supporting the independent position of the Interstate Commerce Commission:

Its most significant tasks involve the adjudication of controversies and the prescription of courses of action for the future. The performance of such tasks necessitates and has in practice been accorded the same thoroughness of consideration and impartiality which are deemed to characterize judicial proceedings. The commission is no

---

[2] See *Washington Daily News*, Nov. 17, 1937. For recent criticism of the National Labor Relations Board see *Pittsburgh Press*, Dec. 7, 1937; *Philadelphia Inquirer*, Dec. 9, 1937; *Cong. Rec.*, 75th Cong., 2nd sess., p. 802; *Cong. Rec.*, 75th Cong., 3rd sess., p. 3194. For recent criticism of the Federal Communications Commission see *Cong. Rec.*, 75th Cong., 1st sess., pp. 659–60, 2332–37, 9141, 9406.

more a part of the national administration—in the sense of being an instrument for furthering the ends of the party in power—than is the Supreme Court, and executive influence is as out of place in the one case as it would be in the other.[3]

When the question of creating the Federal Trade Commission was before Congress, Representative Graham rested his argument for its independence on the same ground when he said: "An industrial commission is not a part of the executive department of the government. It is more nearly related to the judicial function of the government, and I would wish to see the tenure of office made as secure as possible."[4]

Similarly, in supporting the independent position of all of these commissions, Charles A. and William Beard contend that "if there is any reason for taking the federal courts out of presidential politics and making them to some degree independent of the Chief Executive, there are also grounds for throwing similar safeguards around these quasi-judicial commissions."[5]

The Joint Committee on the Reorganization of the Executive Departments of the federal government[6] reiterated the same contention when, with respect to certain suggestions affecting the independence of these commissions in general, it said in its report:

These suggestions may be dismissed with the comment that the principle involved requires the complete independence of all organizations having quasi-judicial functions from even the appearance of arbitrary control. Short of terminating their work altogether there seems to be no alternative to continuing establishments of this type.[7]

---

[3] *The Interstate Commerce Commission*, II, 454.

[4] *Cong. Rec.*, 63rd Cong., 2nd sess., p. 8987.

[5] *The American Leviathan*, pp. 306–7.

[6] This committee made a broad study of the federal administrative organization in 1924.

[7] *H. R. Doc.* 356, p. 27, 68th Cong., 1st sess. See also in this connection Joseph B. Eastman, "The Place of the Independent Commission," *Constitutional Review*, XII, 101.

There would seem to be little question that independence is necessary to secure the most effective exercise of judicial power, if the interests of the individual are to be given particular emphasis in the exercise of this power. But there is a justifiable difference of opinion whether in the exercise of this power the interests of the individual should receive such emphasis. The state of Oregon, as is later pointed out, has very definitely taken the position that in the field of public utility control the judicial power of its Public Utilities Commissioner shall be exercised merely as a means of furthering the public interest or with primary emphasis on the public interest. However, even if it is held that particular emphasis should be placed on the interests of the individual, it is still a question whether independence and board control do lead to the most effective performance of the administrative and policy formulating powers which many of these commissions enjoy. If not, then from the standpoint of organization a separation in the exercise of these powers would seem desirable so that the appropriate principles of organization may be applied in connection with each. The conflicting nature of the responsibilities also seems to make a separation desirable.[8]

For the most effective exercise of administrative power, opinion today almost uniformly favors the principles of subordination and single head control, including both subordination of tenure and decision.[9] In no case has this opinion been substantiated by

---

[8] See below, pp. 77ff.

[9] See Arthur E. Buck, *Administrative Consolidation in State Governments*, pp. 3–4, 29, 37–38; William F. Willoughby, *The Principles of Public Administration*, p. 120; John M. Mathews, *Principles of American State Administration*, pp. 167–69; D. W. Davis (former Governor of Idaho), "How Administrative Control Is Working in Idaho," *National Municipal Review*, VIII, 615–30; Frank O. Lowden (former Governor of Illinois), "Business Government," *Saturday Evening Post*, Mar. 14, 1920; Herbert Hoover, *Hearings before the Joint Committee on Reorganization of the Executive Departments*, 68th Cong., 1st sess., p. 334; *University of Texas Bulletin*, no. 98, citing reports of some thirty state investigating committees.

closely supervised experimentation. But experiments have been made in such a large number of cases and opinion has so generally supported the success of the experiments that there is strong reason for believing that these principles of organization are in fact better for the exercise of administrative powers than independence and board control. These principles of organization, it is generally held, in view of that experience, tend to secure the following results in contrast with the principles of independence and board control: the first is effective integration in the exercise of administrative power, and this is believed to be best attained by resort to both the principle of single head control and the principle of subordination. For, while subordination makes possible a centralized control over the exercise of administrative power, single head control, by making responsibility definite, ensures the most effective exercise of that control. The second result is more rigid attention to duty, which is generally traced to the psychological state of mind induced where the officer is made clearly responsible for action under the principle of single head control and accountable for his action under the principle of subordination, including subordinate tenure. The third and fourth results, generally attributed primarily to the use of single head control, are prompter action and greater economy in organization.

Generally, also, subordination and single head control have been regarded as complementary principles, and it seems evident from the foregoing discussion that there is a very definite interrelationship between them in the sense that one depends upon the other for the fullest realization of its own characteristics.

Recently Professor Carl J. Friedrich has taken the position that equally effective integration in the exercise of administrative powers can be secured without provision for subordinate tenure, and he cites the civil service of the United States and of certain foreign countries as examples.[10]   Whether an equally effective integration can be secured can not, however, be shown by reference to the United States civil service, for the members of that service do not yet enjoy independent tenure.   They are still subject to removal by the heads of the departments, who are incidentally presidential subordinates, for "such cause as will promote the efficiency of the service." [11]   Certain formal restraints, such as notice to civil servants of the causes for their removal, are required.[12]   But it has been specifically held that the department head is the final judge of what shall constitute sufficient causes for removal.[13]   Despite the very general agreement in this country that members of the civil service should be entirely free from partisan influences, it has not yet been found desirable in the federal service to provide them with independent tenure.   In actual practice, a certain tradition has developed under which partisan considerations have been largely eliminated in the exercise of the removal power.[14]   This, however, is by no means the same thing as independent tenure and could never be claimed to have any adverse effect upon the process of integration.

In the second place, Professor Friedrich asserts that more rigid attention to duty can be secured where the officer is given the opportunity to develop a sense of responsibility to professional standards, which he terms "objective" responsibility, instead of being made accountable for his action to a political superior, which he terms "political" responsibility.   Accordingly, he favors provision for comparatively long terms of office and independent tenure under which removals would be restricted by "a rigidly

---

[10] "Responsible Government Service under the American Constitution," in *Problems of the American Public Service* (1935), pp. 34–37.

[11] U. S. Code (1934), Title 5, sec. 652.   [12] *Ibid.*

[13] *Eberlein* v. *U. S.,* 53 Ct. Cl. 466 (1918); *Golding* v. *U. S.,* 78 Ct. Cl. 682 (1934). See also Lewis Mayers, *The Federal Service,* pp. 494–95; Lucius Wilmerding, Jr., *Government by Merit* (1935), p. 224.   [14] Mayers, p. 500.

defined disciplinary procedure." [15]   In contrasting the psychological effect of such provisions with the effect of a subordinate tenure provision, Professor Friedrich says:

> If their [the commissions'] members look upon their governmental service as their life work, they are more likely to pursue its tasks with a view to the general interest for which the service has been established than if they must cultivate outside relationships which will take care of them when they are removed from their public post.   It is this psychological factor which supplements "objective" responsibility. Moreover its force can be greatly enhanced by ensuring a career in the service.   Therefore the possibility of rising within the service on the sole recommendation of meritorious service to some extent produces a responsible governmental service precisely where the patronage destroys it.[16]

As yet, however, Professor Friedrich's position has not apparently been well substantiated by experience in this country, where, including the civil service systems of the states and cities, both independent and subordinate tenure have been tried.   The Commission of Inquiry on Public Service Personnel failed to make any specific recommendations along these lines in its recent report; [17] and, in fact, among the experienced administrators and other competent observers who testified before the commission, a majority were opposed to other than purely formal restrictions on the exercise of the removal power.[18]

---

[15] This phrase may be variously interpreted.   But it seems evident that Professor Friedrich means a procedure under which the removing officer would not be the final judge of causes for removal.

[16] *Op. cit.*, pp. 37–38.   Quoted by permission of the McGraw-Hill Book Co., Inc.

[17] *Better Government Personnel*, Report of the Commission of Inquiry on Public Service Personnel (1935).   The committee's specific recommendations are printed on pp. 4–9.

[18] Minutes of Evidence taken before the Commission of Inquiry on Public Service Personnel (1935).   For those who favored restrictions, see pp. 63–64, 98, 290, 369, 507, 516.   For those opposed, see pp. 186, 205, 263, 315, 367, 381,

Professor Paul T. Stafford has recently claimed that some actual state experience is to be found in which independence and board control have proven superior to subordinate and single head control in the exercise of administrative power.[19] Upon examination, though, it will be found that he offers little convincing evidence to support that position. He cites a report of an investigation committee of California which recommended that the State Department of Social Welfare be abolished and its duties entrusted to the State Board of Control.[20] The committee also recommended, however, that most of the services performed by the department be abolished. Its essential reason for the suggested change was that sufficient welfare duties would not exist to justify continuing the department. It selected the Board of Control, not because of its board organization but because it already existed for other purposes and had previously had experience with welfare work. This was made clear by the committee itself when it said:

Inasmuch as we recommend the elimination of the state supervision of adoptions, the elimination of the state inspection of boarding homes and the elimination of state supervision of probation and jail inspection, the only remaining functions of the department are in connection with aid to the aged, aid to the needy blind, and orphans aid.

Under the plan proposed by the committee the only function of the state in connection with the aid to the aged will be to compute the various proportionate amounts which the counties are entitled to.

With regard to the aid to the needy blind, the services of the Department of Social Welfare have apparently become perfunctory

---

426–27, 472. For others who take the same position, see Mayers, p. 500; Wilmerding, p. 226.

[19] "The New Amateur in Public Administration," *American Political Science Review*, XXIX, 258–61.

[20] The majority of the members of this agency are, however, subordinate to the governor, so that in this instance only the principle of board control was involved. See Political Code of California (1931), I, secs. 655, 656, 663.

and the right of appeal reserved could easily be handled by the State Board of Control. The necessary state control of expenditures for orphans aid, as the committee above stated, could be administered with equal efficiency and much less expense through the State Board of Control as was done prior to 1925.[21]

Taking these facts into consideration, the committee can see no real justification for the continuance of the Department of Social Welfare. . . .[22]

In addition, Professor Stafford cites certain recommendations of an Ohio investigating committee. One of these concerned the State Department of Public Welfare, in place of which the committee recommended that consideration be given to the propriety of creating an independent Board of Public Welfare.[23] But the committee also suggested that it would be desirable to see first what results could be obtained by reorganizing the department itself.[24] Another of the committee's recommendations called for the substitution of board control in place of the existing single head control of the State Department of Public Health.[25] But the committee offered no particular reasons for this step and, in fact, it very strongly commended the record of the department in the following words: "Ohio's expenditures for the State Department of Health are lower than those of any other large state, yet the state ranks among the best in the quality and extent of work done."[26]

Finally, Professor Stafford cites two recent reports of the Institute for Government Research of the Brookings Institution, in which the institute recommended board control for public welfare

---

[21] Under the committee's proposed plan most of this work was to be performed by the counties with the Board of Control merely enjoying the routine function of checking applications for aid approved by the counties.

[22] *Final Report of the Fact-Finding Committee of the Senate*, California Legislature (1933), p. 13.

[23] *Report of the Ohio Joint Committee on Economy in the Public Service* (1929), pp. 11–12.   [24] *Ibid.*, p. 9.   [25] *Ibid.*, p. 142.   [26] *Ibid.*, p. 136.

administration in Iowa [27] and Mississippi.[28]   Neither of these steps, however, represented changes from single head to board control.   For, at the time of the recommendations, Iowa was employing merely a temporary committee for welfare administration while Mississippi's welfare administration was scattered among a variety of boards.   Furthermore, the institute specifically proposed, in connection with each report, that a single commissioner be employed by the board for the exercise of its executive or administrative powers and that the board confine itself to the formulation of welfare policy.[29]   These boards, moreover, and hence the commissioners, were subordinated to the governor both in tenure and decision.

Neither Professor Friedrich nor Professor Stafford seems, then, to discredit the prevailing opinion based on considerable though not closely supervised experimentation, according to which subordination and single head control is favored for the exercise of administrative powers.

Where, however, policy formulating powers are to be exercised, opinion in this country has predominantly favored the principles of independence and board control.[30]   In accordance with that opinion, the only suggestion that has usually been made is to entrust the administrative powers of these commissions to subordinate single head agencies, such as divisions within the appropriate executive departments.[31]   This would seem to be desirable

---

[27] *Report on a Survey of Administration in Iowa* (1933), pp. 238–39.

[28] *Report on a Survey of the Organization and Administration of State and County Government in Mississippi* (1932), p. 562.

[29] In connection with Iowa, see p. 53 of the *Report*.   In connection with Mississippi, see *Summary of the Facts, Findings and Recommendations of a Report on a Survey of State and County Government in Mississippi,* prepared by the institute (1932), p. 59.

[30] This position is taken by practically all of those cited in note 9 of this chapter.

[31] See, for example, W. F. Willoughby, *The Principles of Public Administration,* p. 120; Herbert Hoover, *Hearings before the Joint Committee on Reorganization of the Executive Departments,* 68th Cong., 1st sess., pp. 334–35.

where these commissions have no policy formulating powers.[82] But where they have been entrusted with policy formulating power, many of the advantages now derived from a union between policy formulation and administrative action[83] would be lost if they were deprived of their administrative powers. Hence, in the organization of these particular commissions, a certain dilemma is presented so long as it is believed that they should, nevertheless, continue to operate as independent and board control units because of their policy formulating powers. In any event, it is important to consider whether independence and board control seem in fact necessary for an effective exercise of policy formulating power. This belief has not yet been founded on actual experience. Almost uniformly in both federal and state practice the necessity for those principles of organization has been assumed. Nevertheless, there are, at present, two noteworthy instances in which both subordination and single head control are actually being employed in connection with this type of power.

The first is represented by the Bureau of Animal Industry in the Department of Agriculture, which has been entrusted by the secretary of that department with the administration of the Packers and Stockyards Act. This act provides for an exercise of wide discretionary powers with respect to the operations and practices of packers, market agencies, and dealers, and the rates, operations, and practices of stockyards. These discretionary powers, moreover, are as broad as those entrusted to any of the commissions. Thus, in the matter of rates to be charged by stockyards, the act empowers the secretary to determine what rates are "just and reasonable,"[34] while, with respect to the prac-

---

[82] As the Employees Compensation Commission, the National Labor Relations Board, and the Social Security Board.

[83] For a later discussion of this point, see pp. 71–72.

[34] 42 Stat. L. 159, sec. 310.

tices of both packers and stockyards, it empowers him to determine what practices are "unfair, unjustly discriminatory or deceptive." [35]

Prior to the passage of the act, a very strong effort was made in Congress to entrust its administration to an independent commission, to be known as the Federal Livestock Commission, or, at least, to an independent commissioner. But largely because of the opposition of the House to either proposal the secretary of Agriculture was finally selected for the work.[36] The secretary first entrusted administration of the act to an agency called the Packers and Stockyards Administration. Later he selected the Bureau of Animal Industry for the task because of its related activities.[37] This bureau is headed by a single individual who is completely subordinate in tenure and decision to the secretary of Agriculture and hence to the president.

A more instructive experiment, perhaps, has been going on in Oregon since the creation in 1931 of the office of Public Utilities Commissioner of Oregon.[38] For prior to the creation of this agency, Oregon had experimented first with the principles of independence and board control in the form of the Oregon Railroad Commission, and, secondly, with the principles of subordination and board control in the form of the Oregon Public Service Commission.[39] The policy formulating power that has been

---

[35] *Ibid.*, sec. 202–3, 312.

[36] See *Cong. Rec.*, 66th Cong., 3rd sess., pp. 45, 1870–71, 1875; *Cong. Rec.*, 67th Cong., 1st sess., pp. 2319, 2379, 2701, 2709–13.

[37] Department of Agriculture, *Annual Reports* (1928), p. 47.

[38] Oregon Laws (1931), ch. 103, sec. 1. The commissioner is made completely subordinate to the governor in section 2 of the act. This section provides that the governor may remove the commissioner "for any cause deemed by him to be sufficient and such power of removal shall be absolute and there shall be no right of review of the same in any court whatsoever."

[39] This commission was not, however, as completely subordinate to the governor as the present Public Utilities Commissioner. For, while the governor was made the final judge in his exercise of the removal power with respect to its

entrusted to the Public Utilities Commissioner is as broad as that entrusted to any of these commissions and extends over a wider range of economic activity than even the power of the Interstate Commerce Commission. Thus the commissioner has been vested with control over the rates, rules, and practices of every public utility in the state including railroads, street railroads, motor vehicles, water, gas, electric light and power companies, telephone companies, and telegraph companies.[40]

The act creating the office of Public Utilities Commissioner was passed largely at the instance of Governor Julius L. Meier, although there had been a growing dissatisfaction with the work of the Public Service Commission, as there had been with its predecessor, the Railroad Commission. That dissatisfaction had, in fact, become so strong in 1925 that Governor Walter M. Pierce had asked the legislature to make no further appropriations for the existing commission.[41]

In recommending both single head control and more complete subordination, Governor Meier said:

At present in this state there is no real competition among public utilities even though engaged in the same line of business. In fields where two or more utilities offer the same type of service, competition is effectively prevented by regulation of the Public Service Commission and by agreement between the utilities or both. . . . With the personnel of the commission I have no quarrel, as the regulatory machinery under which it operates has imposed upon it a task impossible of performance.

Because regulation as it now exists in this state has proven an utter failure, I recommend abolition of the Public Service Commission as

---

members, he was authorized to remove them only for "inefficiency, neglect of duty or malfeasance in office." See Code of 1930, secs. 61–102.

[40] Code of 1930, sec. 61–206, 207, transferred to the Public Utilities Commissioner by sec. 2 of Oregon Laws (1931).

[41] *Message of Walter M. Pierce, Governor of Oregon, to the Thirty-First Legislative Assembly* (1925), p. 12.

now constituted and the creation of a Department of Public Utilities
to consist of a single commissioner, appointed by and removable at the
discretion of the Governor. . . .[42]

A general survey will show that both the Bureau of Animal
Industry and the Public Utilities Commissioner of Oregon have
performed their tasks in commendable fashion. However, only
the Public Utilities Commissioner had been preceded by an independent commission with substantially similar tasks and thus
made possible a contrast in principles of organization. But, unfortunately, this experiment has not been so supervised as to
justify definite conclusions respecting the superiority of subordination and single head control where policy formulating as well
as other powers are to be exercised. However, it is worth pointing out that the office of Public Utilities Commissioner of Oregon
has so far escaped the criticism leveled against its predecessors and
that, during the first four years of its operation it effected savings
for the public amounting to nearly three million dollars in railroad and other utility rates.[43] Further it is worth pointing out
that the bulk of these savings were effected without resort to the
courts.[44]

While neither of these experiments justify positive conclusions
respecting the relative merits of independent board control organization and subordinate single head control organization
where policy formulating powers are to be exercised, they have at
least served to refute some of the arguments frequently advanced
in favor of independence and board control. These arguments
will now be examined.

Independence, it has at times been asserted, ensures greater
objectivity or impartiality in the exercise of the broad discre-

[42] *Inaugural Message of Julius L. Meier, Governor of Oregon, to the Thirty-
Sixth Legislative Assembly* (1931), p. 4.

[43] *Report of the Office of Public Utilities Commissioner of Oregon* (1935), p. 1.

[44] *Ibid.*

tionary powers of policy formulation than where the principle of subordination is used.[45] Independence of tenure is also regarded as indispensable to any real position of independence, as obviously it must be.[46] Further, this objectivity is sometimes held to be of particular importance on the ground that it makes possible a scientific determination of governmental policy.[47]

There can be no question that independence of thought and action is necessary to the fullest attainment of objectivity. But it may be seriously questioned whether anything approaching real objectivity and hence anything approaching a scientific determination can be expected in policy formulation, whatever the principles of organization. For in the field of policy formulation broad social and economic objectives are involved, and, in consequence, the substitution of the principle of subordination for independence is likely to mean no more than the substitution of the social or economic objectives of a class of individuals, operating as a party, for the social or economic objectives of a few individuals. This is not to deny the importance of an expert and scientific determination of facts to form the basis for the exercise of the policy formulating powers of these commissions as, for example, the determination of just and reasonable rates. It is simply to assert that this factual information will seldom be the sole basis for the final determination, but consciously or not will be used in furtherance of economic and social objectives. However such expert factual information is obviously essential for an intelligent realization of these objectives.

The most objectivity that it seems reasonable to expect in the field of policy formulation is freedom from discrimination against

---

[45] See Marshall E. Dimock, "The Prospect for Administrative Tribunals," *California Law Review*, XX, 166; Gerard C. Henderson, *The Federal Trade Commission*, p. 341; Friedrich, p. 34.

[46] For an earlier discussion of this point see above p. 16.

[47] See Friedrich, p. 34; Henderson, p. 341.

particular individuals or groups because of their partisan connections. But the two experiments just noted, the Federal Bureau
of Animal Industry and the Public Utilities Commissioner of
Oregon, seem to show that this freedom from discrimination is
not an attribute of independence alone. Both of these agencies
have shown a very commendable spirit of fairness in their action,
nor has any of their action yet been criticized on the ground of
partisan discrimination. Perhaps these experiments show that,
in the field of policy formulation where the very broadness of the
discretionary power places its exercise in the forefront of public
attention, a fair substitute for independence may be found in the
principle of definite responsibility which single head control ensures. In one of its many surveys of state administration, the
Institute for Government Research of the Brookings Institution
says: "When important responsibilities are definitely located in
an office, the office tends to become individualized and, because
the attention of the people is centered upon it, the individual
holding that office is often disposed to rise above personal and
narrowly partisan considerations." [48]

At the same time, the subordinate status of the Federal Bureau
of Animal Industry and the Public Utilities Commissioner of
Oregon make it possible to secure an effective integration between
their policy and the broad lines of policy developed by the president or the governor, as the case may be. The full importance of
integration in policy formulation has not been generally recognized because of a failure to appreciate the very definite interrelationship that exists in the many economic and social problems
for which governmental policy as a whole must be devised.
Without constant regard for this interrelationship no effective
approach can be made to those problems either individually or as

---

[48] *Report on a Survey of Administration in Iowa,* submitted to the Committee
on Reductions of Governmental Expenditures by the Institute for Governmental
Research of the Brookings Institution (1933), p. 81.

a whole. In other words, integration in the formulation of policy is a method of approach that corresponds to economic and social realities. In 1921 the actual interrelationship between agriculture, industry, and transportation was presented by the Joint Committee on Agricultural Inquiry in an able study,[49] and more recently the question of interrelationship has also been emphasized in connection with these commissions.[50] In a situation, therefore, where various administrative agencies are engaged in the formulation of policy, conflicts are bound to develop; and no effective way exists for terminating these conflicts unless the agencies are subject to a common direction.

There have been numerous conflicts in policy between these commissions themselves or these commissions and federal departments. In his study of the Federal Trade Commission, Thomas C. Blaisdell cites many conflicts between the commission and the Department of Justice. In one instance according to Blaisdell:

The commissioners [Federal Trade] . . . endeavored to arbitrate the price of newsprint paper so far as to provide for paper publishers not protected by contracts. The attempt failed when indictments for violations of the anti-trust laws were brought by the Attorney-General against certain members of the Manufacturers' Association, who were also parties to the arbitration proceeding.[51]

Two very recent conflicts may also be cited. In December, 1937 the National Bituminous Coal Commission proceeded to set the

[49] *H. R. Rep.* 408, Vol. III, Part 3, Ch. I, 67th Cong., 1st sess.

[50] See testimony of C. E. McGuire, *Hearings of the Joint Committee on Reorganization of the Executive Departments*, p. 246, 68th Cong., 1st sess.; Frederick A. Cleveland, "The Reorganization of the Federal Government," *Proceedings of the American Academy of Political Science*, IX, 374; James Hart, "The President and Federal Administration," in *Essays on the Law and Practice of Governmental Administration*, p. 77; E. Pendleton Herring, "Politics, Personalities and the Federal Trade Commission," *American Political Science Review*, XXIX, 32, 35.

[51] Reprinted from Blaisdell, *The Federal Trade Commission*, pp. 154–55. Quoted by permission of Columbia University Press. For other instances cited see pp. 200–3, 218–19, 242–43, 282–83.

prices of coal so high as to seriously threaten the rate structure developed by the Interstate Commerce Commission.[52] In June, 1938 a very fundamental conflict developed between the Board of Governors of the Federal Reserve System, on the one hand, and the Department of the Treasury, the Comptroller of the Currency, and the Federal Deposit Insurance Corporation on the other hand. The immediate issue concerned the liberalization of bank examining principles, but it reached the fundamental question of how credit should be liberalized to stimulate recovery.[53]

In many cases, of course, some degree of co-ordination between the departments and these commissions or between the commissions themselves has been effected. In a recent congressional hearing Acting Chairman Sykes of the Federal Communications Commission testified that the commission had encountered no difficulty in securing the co-operation of the departments of State, War, Navy, Commerce, and Justice.[54] If co-ordination is to continue to rest on a voluntary basis, it would greatly facilitate the process if, as proposed by Professor Beard,[55] a joint standing committee of Congress were established with responsibility for keeping all policy formulating agencies continually informed of the various lines of policy being developed elsewhere.

But the fullest measure of co-ordination can not be attained so long as it rests on a voluntary basis. For many conflicts in the formulation of policy will undoubtedly be generated by fundamental differences in social and economic objectives; and these differences, it may be expected, will also in many cases be too strongly held to make mutual information effective. For the

---

[52] See *United States News,* March 7, 1938, p. 3. Fortunately these prices were rescinded two months later.

[53] *Ibid.,* June 20, 1938, p. 13. See also *The Evening Sun* (Baltimore), June 17, 1938, p. 2.

[54] *Hearings before the Joint Committee on Government Organization,* 75th Cong., 1st sess., p. 199.

[55] For a full discussion of this proposal see below pp. 73–74.

most effective co-ordination, therefore, these commissions along with the other policy formulating units of the administration should be subject to a common direction; and the president is the logical one to exercise this power of direction, since he is already the head of the greater part of the administration and the recognized leader in the field of national policy. Furthermore, these commissions should be subordinated to the president in tenure as well as decision if the fullest measure of subordination is to be made possible. He should be able to have on these commissions men of his own way of thinking or with his own social and economic objectives, and to remove those no longer of his own way of thinking.

In support of the principle of board control in connection with the exercise of policy formulating power, particular emphasis has generally been placed upon the thoroughness of consideration to be expected from provision for collective and representative judgment.[56] Occasionally some emphasis has also been placed upon the continuity of experience which board control tends to provide where, as in the case of all of these commissions, the terms of their members are staggered so as to provide a continuing personnel.[57] It seems evident, though, that this element of experience could be just as well supplied by the subordinate officials employed by the commission and that it can hardly furnish much justification for board control. Greater continuity of decision rather than of experience, though one often accompanies the

---

[56] See W. F. Willoughby, *The Principles of Public Administration*, p. 122; *Report of the Special Committee on Trust Legislation of the U. S. Chamber of Commerce*, April 14, 1914, cited in *Cong. Rec.*, 63rd Cong., 2nd sess., p. 8841; Senator Hitchcock, *ibid.*, p. 851; Charles W. Needham, "Judicial Determinations by Administrative Commissions," *American Political Science Review*, X, 240–41.

[57] See statement by Senator Newlands, *Cong. Rec.*, 63rd Cong., 2nd sess., p. 11083. Howell Ellis (member of the Public Service Commission of Indiana), "Four Reasons Why I Question the One-man Commission Idea," *Public Utilities Fortnightly*, IX, 159.

other, or less abrupt changes in governmental policy toward those
subject to commission regulation than could be assured under
single head control, would seem to furnish a more substantial
justification. For, without some such assurance against abrupt
changes in governmental policy, it may be asserted, those subject
to commission regulation would not engage in their normal
economic or business activity. Emphasizing the importance of
continuity in this sense, Professor Ernst Freund says: "Variability
. . . is desirable only in a very few phases of economic or social
regulation. What industry needs above all is permanence and
continuity of policy and requirement." [58]

There can be little question that thorough consideration and a
reasonable continuity of action are necessary to any effective
exercise of policy formulating power. But the operation of the
Bureau of Animal Industry since 1927, when it was entrusted
with administration of the Packers and Stockyards Act, and the
operation of the Public Utilities Commissioner of Oregon since
1931, when the office was created, seem to show that both of these
characteristics may be attained under single head control. In
respect to thoroughness of consideration, both of these agencies
have frequently conducted investigation for two and even three
years before taking action.[59] That they have also maintained a
sufficient continuity of decision is evident from the fact that there
has been as yet no noticeable lessening in the economic or business
activity of those subject to their regulation. Perhaps here again
the definite responsibility of single head control and the very
broadness of the power to be exercised, placing it in the forefront

---

[58] "The Substitution of Rule for Discretion in Public Law," *American Political Science Review*, IX, 668. It has also been claimed that board control offers a better guarantee of independence on the ground that it is more difficult for the president to influence a group of individuals than a single individual. See *Cong. Rec.*, 63rd Cong., 2nd sess., pp. 678, 680, 964.

[59] See, for example, *Report of the Office of Public Utilities Commissioner of Oregon* (1935), pp. 8–10; Bureau of Animal Industry, Docket nos. 311, 344.

of public attention, has proved a fitting substitute for the characteristics of board control.

At the same time these agencies retain, by reason of their single head control, the power to act both promptly and vigorously when prompt and vigorous action is required. The full significance of this aspect of single head control in the field of policy formulation is not usually appreciated. Generally, the problem of securing action where board control is employed in policy formulation is believed to be no more serious than where it is employed in connection with the exercise of administrative power. In actual fact, the problem is a much more serious one. In the exercise of administrative power so little discretion is involved that serious differences of opinion among the members of an agency respecting particular courses of action will seldom develop. But in the exercise of policy formulating powers differences of opinion serious enough to obstruct action are at times inevitable, for broad social and economic objectives are involved.

Such differences of opinion existed for some time among the members of the Federal Trade Commission [60] and were perhaps among the principal causes of the general lack of dispatch with which it has been so frequently charged.[61] Such differences of opinion have also existed among the members of the National Bituminous Coal Commission which has been criticized more severely for inaction than any of these commissions.[62] On December 16, 1937 this commission, after a period of little apparent activity, began to fix the prices of soft coal.[63] Two months later it rescinded these prices.[64] The dissension that has existed within

---

[60] See *Annual Report* of the Federal Trade Commission (1925), pp. 111, 117, 199–201, 208–11, 214–18.

[61] See Myron W. Watkins, "The Federal Trade Commission; A Critical Survey," *Quarterly Journal of Economics*, XL, 580–82; Henderson, pp. 86 ff.; Blaisdell, pp. 86–91.

[62] See footnotes 1 and 2, of this chapter.

[63] *United States News*, March 7, 1938, p. 3.   [64] *Ibid.*

the commission has recently been brought to light following the resignation of its Acting Director of Trial Examiners.[65] Dissension has also apparently existed among the members of the Federal Communications Commission.[66]

It would seem more difficult, therefore, to obtain action in the exercise of policy formulating powers than in the exercise of administrative powers where a board instead of a single head is employed, and yet the need for action is equally if not more pressing in the field of policy formulation than in the field of administrative action. For the social scene to which policy must be adapted is not static but in a process of continual and very rapid change. In criticizing public utility regulation in this country, a recent British critic says:

The great difficulties in which the United States has been involved in these twenty years to evolve a workable system of control which will do more good than harm have been due very largely to the want of elasticity in the methods adopted. The decisions of the commissions and of the courts have so often been too late; circumstances have changed while the parties and experts have been talking.[67]

At times it has been claimed that both independence and board control tend to inspire greater confidence among those particularly affected by commission action, as well as among the public generally. Professor William O. Weyforth, in supporting the independence of the Board of Governors of the Federal Reserve System, says that "the confidence of the banking and business community in the reserve system is likely to be weakened if there are grounds for believing that the credit policy has been domi-

---

[65] *Washington Daily News,* Nov. 17, 1937.

[66] See Harold Brayman, "The FPC, the FCC, the SEC," *Public Utilities Fortnightly,* XVIII (July, 1936), 115.

[67] Sir H. N. Bunbury, K.C.B., "The Economic Regulation of Public Utilities," *Public Administration,* IV, 211.

nated by political considerations." [68]   In connection with the board control of the Federal Trade Commission, Representative Towner said, in arguing for an even larger membership than was originally proposed: "A commission composed of three men is, in the eyes of the people, almost a committee. The hearings before three men will be by no means as impressive as those before five. It will greatly dignify this commission if it shall be composed of the number of men that almost every one of us realizes ought to compose it." [69]

Lack of confidence in the action of these commissions, especially on the part of those directly affected by their action, would undoubtedly have serious consequences for the success of their regulatory efforts. But such a condition has clearly not developed with respect to either the action of the Bureau of Animal Industry or the Public Utilities Commissioner of Oregon and there seems little reason why that condition should develop so long as these agencies continue efficient and conscientious service. For after all it is the standard of performance rather than the characteristics of organization that determines the public confidence in which any governmental agency will be held. Certainly, despite its organization, the National Bituminous Coal Commission has deserved little public confidence.

As was earlier pointed out, the United States Tariff Commission and the National Mediation Board, though entrusted with powers that fall within the general category of administrative powers, have generally been regarded as desirable exceptions from the opinion favoring subordination and single head control where

---

[68] *The Federal Reserve Board*, p. 198. The term "political" is ambiguous. It is apparently used here to mean "partisan." See also in connection with the Federal Trade Commission, Representative Morgan, *Cong. Rec.*, 63rd Cong., 2nd sess., p. 8857; *H. R. Rep.* 533, 63rd Cong., 2nd sess., p. 3.

[69] *Cong. Rec.*, 63rd Cong., 2nd sess., p. 8986. See also *Hearings before the Select Committee on Government Organization, United States Senate*, 75th Cong., 1st sess., pp. 207, 208, 229.

administrative powers are to be exercised. Whether they seem to be desirable exceptions is the question for discussion here.

Where merely the power of investigation is to be exercised it would seem that the only possible justification for independence is impartiality or objectivity and that the only possible justification for board control is the more effective guarantee of independence that it might provide. Neither of the other characteristics associated with board control, collective and representative judgment and continuity, are of much real importance in the exercise of this class of action. Some discretion is of course involved in the interpretation of data, but it is hardly broad enough to furnish an argument for collective judgment. Nor would there seem to be any necessity for having any greater continuity of action than the subordinate officials of the agency will provide. On the other hand, all of the characteristics associated with subordination and single head control would seem to be desirable for this class of action.

There can be no doubt that questions relating to the tariff, insofar as they have a direct bearing upon tariff rates, are matters where impartiality is particularly difficult to obtain. For tariff rates have been a constant source of partisan conflict. This was the general reason urged both in and outside of Congress for the creation of the United States Tariff Commission as an independent board control agency.[70] The claim was made that the commission would, either because of its own reputation for impartiality or because of the impartial information provided the electorate, exert a healthy influence in the determination of tariff rates. Such an influence, however, has not yet been apparent. Unquestionably the commission has had a certain influence with

---

[70] See, for example, Referendum No. 2 on the Question of a Permanent Tariff Commission, sent by the U. S. Chamber of Commerce to its members in 1913, cited in "Tariff Making—Discussion," *American Economic Review*, XVI, supp., p. 199. See also *Cong. Rec.*, 64th Cong., 1st sess., pp. 10612, 13801, 13820.

respect to tariff legislation; instances in which its influence has been unmistakable can be cited.[71]   But they all involve minor aspects of the tariff question, such as forms of classification, which would not, in any event, have been the subject of partisan conflict and which might, therefore, have been just as impartially performed by a subordinate single head unit.   In matters having a direct bearing upon rates, where the real danger of partisanship exists, the commission appears to have had little or no influence, and this has been recognized even by members of the commission itself.[72]

Mr. Thomas W. Page, a former commissioner, attributes this failure of the commission in part to its practice of merely supplying the political organs with an array of facts without indicating the significance of those facts in terms of particular rates. But he admits, also, that a more fundamental cause for its failure has been the unwillingness of the political organs to forego partisan considerations; [73] and he sees little hope for any real increase in its influence unless the public will, on the basis of its investigations, exert a coercive influence upon the action of the political organs.[74]   To expect the public, however, to begin in the near future to exert any such influence seems altogether impractical, and, if the development of that condition is essential to the commission's influence, there would seem to be little justification for continuing it as an independent board-controlled unit.

Professor Frank Taussig and Mr. Edward P. Costigan, both

---

[71] See, for example, *H. R. Rep.* 248, 67th Cong., 1st sess., p. 3.   See also the following annual reports of the commission: *Sixth Annual Report*, pp. 10–13; *Eleventh Annual Report*, p. 14; *Thirteenth Annual Report*, pp. 12–15; *Fourteenth Annual Report*, p. 15.

[72] See Thomas W. Page, *Making the Tariff in the United States*, p. 30; Frank W. Taussig, "The United States Tariff Commission and the Tariff," *American Economic Review*, XVI, supp., p. 177; "Tariff Making—Discussion," *American Economic Review*, XVI, supp., p. 200.

[73] Page, p. 38.   [74] *Ibid.*, p. 174.

former members of the commission, believe, on the other hand, that the principal reason for its failure has been presidential interference or attempts to influence its action.[75] This interference, they believe, has detracted from the commission's influence because it has prevented the commission from acquiring an atmosphere of complete impartiality.[76] That this rather than the unwillingness of Congress to forego partisan considerations in tariff making has been the real cause of the commission's failure, may well be doubted since the tariff has been a partisan issue in Congress for so many years. But, until the commission has attained complete freedom from such interference, no conclusion with respect to its independent and board control organization is possible.

Where merely the power of mediation is to be exercised, there seems little justification for the principles of independence and board control. In fact, while Congress has applied these principles in connection with railroad labor disputes, it has applied the opposing principles, in the establishment of a division in the Department of Labor, for labor disputes in general. In 1917, the secretary of Labor stated his belief that no substantial reason could be found for using an independent commission for mediatory action in the following passage:

There appears to be no logical reason for this segregation of effort. The work of the Board of Mediation and Conciliation[77] is not essentially different, in scope, purpose or method, from the broad general function delegated to the Department of Labor under sections 1 and 8 of its organic act. The industrial problems involved and the plan of procedure necessary to their solution are in no wise different, and it is therefore believed that the organization and func-

---

[75] For examples of this interference, see above p. 17.

[76] Taussig, *op. cit.*, p. 177; "Tariff Making—Discussion," *American Economic Review,* XVI, supp., p. 200.

[77] One of the predecessors of the National Mediation Board.

tions of the Board of Mediation and Conciliation should be transferred to the Department of Labor, and with the organization already existing within this department, should form the Division of Conciliation in the office of the Secretary of Labor.[78]

In 1921, the National Budget Committee of New York City also recommended this step,[79] as did another secretary of Labor in 1924.[80]

On the other hand, it has been frequently maintained that the assurance of impartiality supposedly conveyed where the principles of independence and board control are employed is indispensable in mediatory action because indispensable to the confidence of the parties in conflict. Mr. George A. Barnett and Mr. David A. McCabe take this position in their work on industrial disputes.[81] The same position was also very definitely taken by two of the nine members of the United States Commission on Industrial Relations [82] and by its Director of Research and Investigation. The director even went so far as to recommend that the existing mediatory action of the Department of Labor be entrusted, along with mediatory action in railway disputes, to a new independent commission to be known as the National Mediation Commission.[83] This recommendation, however, was not supported by any of the commissioners; in fact, three of them very definitely opposed it.[84]

---

[78] Letter transmitted to the Speaker of the House of Representatives by the secretary of Labor, Department of Labor, *Annual Report* (1917), p. 101.

[79] "Proposed Reorganization of the Federal Executive Departments," *New York Times*, June 14, 1921.

[80] *Hearings of Joint Committee on the Reorganization of the Executive Departments*, 68th Cong., 1st sess., p. 633. It should be pointed out that both secretaries of Labor may have been influenced by a desire to increase their jurisdiction.

[81] *Mediation, Investigation and Arbitration in Industrial Disputes*, pp. 142–44.

[82] *Final Report of the Commission on Industrial Relations*, Sen. Doc. 415, Vol. I, 64th Cong., 1st sess., p. 186.

[83] *Ibid.*, p. 121.   [84] *Ibid.*, pp. 156, 164.

In 1924 both the Joint Committee on Reorganization of the Executive Departments [85] and President Harding and his cabinet [86] favored continuing the principles of independence and board control in connection with mediatory action in railway labor disputes, although they supported that position with the meaningless assertion that such work is "quasi-judicial."

The principal criticism of the position of those who stress the need for an assurance of nonpartisanship in this class of action is the undue emphasis placed upon that characteristic. The parties in dispute are not bound to accept the recommendations of the mediatory agency, and whether they accept will depend primarily upon the character of the solution offered rather than the source from which it emanates. Partisan or nonpartisan, the organ of mediation will be successful only insofar as it meets the demands of the parties in conflict and no further. This would also seem to apply with equal force to an attempt to justify the use of board control for this class of action as a means of providing the disputing parties with representation on the organ of mediation.

This analysis finds some support in the comparison that follows between the general success that has attended the mediatory efforts of a subordinate single head agency, the Division of Conciliation of the Department of Labor, and the two predecessors of the National Mediation Board, the United States Board of Mediation and Conciliation and the United States Board of Mediation.[87] The comparison only includes the number of instances in which the Division of Conciliation and the boards were actually successful or unsuccessful in their mediatory efforts. It does not include instances where disputes were either aban-

---

[85] *H. R. Doc.* 356, 68th Cong., 1st sess., p. 24.

[86] Cited *ibid.,* appendix a, p. 35.

[87] The Railway Labor Board, which existed from 1920–1926, was also a predecessor of the National Mediation Board, but it was empowered to decide disputes and was not therefore simply| an organ of mediation. 41 Stat. L. 469, sec. 301.

doned or settled by the disputing parties before mediatory efforts were started.

1913–1919	SUCCESS-FUL	UNSUC-CESSFUL	PERCENTAGE OF SUCCESS
U. S. Board of Mediation and Conciliation [88]	91	3	96
Division of Conciliation [89]	2,568	266	90
1926–1933			
U. S. Board of Mediation [90]	914	293	75
Division of Conciliation [91]	3,272	351	90

These figures seem to indicate that, on the whole, slightly greater success has attended the efforts of a subordinate single head agency than those of a commission in the field of federal mediatory action. No such comparison can be very conclusive, however, because of obvious variations in the types of controversies and the personnel engaged in the mediatory efforts.

By way of summary, it would appear that the policy formulating and administrative powers of these commissions with the possible exception of the powers of the United States Tariff Commission might be more effectively exercised if the principles of subordination and single head control were used. This would also seem to be true of their judicial powers provided these powers are to be exercised simply in furtherance of the public interest or with primary emphasis on the public interest. But if their judicial powers are to be exercised with particular attention to the interest of the individual, the principles of independence and board control or at least independence would seem desirable;

---

[88] *Report of the Commissioner of Mediation on the Operations of the U. S. Board of Mediation and Conciliation* (1919), pp. 24–25.

[89] Department of Labor, *Annual Reports* (1921), p. 13.

[90] U. S. Board of Mediation, *Annual Report* (1933), pp. 6–7.

[91] Department of Labor, *Annual Reports* (1933), p. 13.

and accordingly it would seem desirable to separate the judicial powers from the other powers of these commissions so that the appropriate principles of organization might be applied.[92] Additional reasons for effecting this separation if their judicial powers are to be so exercised are discussed among other questions in the following chapter.

---

[92] In his study for the President's Committee on Administrative Management, Professor Robert E. Cushman suggests that the policy formulating and administrative powers of these commissions be entrusted to subordinate single head agencies within the appropriate departments and that their judicial powers be entrusted to independent units which would be organized under the departments for housekeeping purposes only. See *The Problem of the Independent Regulatory Commission*, January, 1937, pp. 26–28.

CHAPTER FOUR

Administrative Exercise of Policy Formulating and Judicial Powers

AS ALREADY pointed out, all of these commissions have been entrusted with administrative powers, and most of them have also been entrusted with policy formulating and judicial powers. Further, where they have also been entrusted with judicial as well as policy formulating powers, almost all of them have been required to proceed in the bulk of their action by a process of adjudication. At the same time, however, they have the administrative responsibility for initiating action or complaints leading to their exercise of judicial power.[1] The significance of the union of powers thus represented and the accompanying procedural requirements will be discussed in this chapter.

In certain fields of commission jurisdiction, as the practices of security exchanges, provision for the exercise of administrative power is in itself significant; for it represents in effect a declaration by the government that such practices are no longer of concern to private individuals only but to the public as well, and that the government will see to it that the public shall at all times have an agency for instituting legal proceedings in the public interest.

---

[1] With the exception of the Employees Compensation Commission. See above p. 13.

Of much greater significance, however, is the delegation to most of these commissions of broad policy formulating and judicial powers in addition to administrative powers. These delegations are not without significance in the field of constitutional jurisprudence, but they are of much greater significance in the field of practical government; and it is accordingly from that standpoint that their principal implications will be examined.

In general, little concern has been shown over the delegations of policy formulating power. The assumption by government of many new responsibilities in comparatively recent years has brought it face to face with a mass of new problems. These problems, moreover, are so numerous, so dynamic and so intricate that they could not be regulated in detail by Congress, a body already overburdened, meeting periodically, and composed of popular representatives having no intimate familiarity with the problems themselves. To expect such a body, for example, to have the time or the expert factual information for determining what railroad rates shall be just and reasonable is to expect the impossible. Such factual information will not in all probability be the sole factor in the determination, as was earlier discussed. Social and economic objectives will be an equally and perhaps more important factor. However this factual information is indispensable to an intelligent realization of these objectives.

But the factual situations of these problems are not only intricate. They are also in a process of dynamic change, and the continual alterations in governmental policy thus made necessary can clearly not be undertaken by Congress, aside from its periodic sessions. In justifying a broad delegation of policy formulating power, a committee of the House of Representatives said in a recent report:

The bill legislates specifically just as far as the committee feels it can. The original bill submitted to the committee dealt very specifically and definitely with a number of admitted abuses. In many cases, however, the argument was made that, while the solutions offered might be correct, their effects were so far reaching as to make it inadvisable to put these solutions in the form of statutory enactments that could not be changed in case of need without congressional action. . . . In a field where practices constantly vary and where practices legitimate for some purposes may be turned to illegitimate and fraudulent means, broad discretionary power in the administrative agency has been found practically essential, despite the desire of the committee to limit the discretion of the administrative agencies so far as compatible with workable legislation.[2]

In 1931 a conference of leaders of the Progressive party [3] met in Washington to consider among other things these broad delegations of policy formulating power. But it failed to consider this problem in all of its aspects. It assumed that Congress had sufficient aptitude for making these determinations and considered the whole problem to be how Congress might restore to itself a greater participation in them.[4]

One year later a British committee, known as the Committee on Ministers' Powers of Great Britain, met and considered that problem in all of its aspects. Its conclusion was that the exercise of such powers by administrative authorities is indispensable to effective governmental regulation of the conditions faced by modern governments today; [5] and this, in fact appears to be the general consensus of opinion both in this country and in England.[6]

---

[2] H. R. Rep. 1383, 73rd Cong., 2nd sess., pp. 6–7. See also John P. Comer, *Legislative Functions of National Administrative Authorities*, p. 16; Joseph B. Eastman, "The Place of the Independent Commission," *Constitutional Review*, XII, 97; *Cong. Rec.*, 67th Cong., 1st sess., p. 1887.

[3] Otherwise known as the Progressive Group in the Republican party.

[4] See *New York Times*, March 12, 1931, p. 21.

[5] *Report of the Committee on Ministers' Powers, presented by the Lord High Chancellor to Parliament,* April, 1932. The committee did, however, suggest one particular safeguard which is later considered.

[6] See John M. Gaus, "The New Problem of Administration," *Minnesota Law Review*, VIII, 217; Comer, p. 16; John B. Cheadle, "The Delegation of Legislative

But while these delegations of policy formulating power seem indispensable to intelligent governmental action, there are certain improvements that might be made in the present manner in which they are being exercised. The first is some provision by which Congress might restore in part, at least, that degree of integration in determinations of policy which is possible when Congress itself makes the determinations and unlikely when some of these determinations are distributed among a number of units.[7]

The simplest and most effective provision for this purpose, and one that has already been discussed, would be subordination of these commissions in tenure and decision to the president. Pending a step of this sort, it would at least seem desirable for Congress to establish a joint standing committee responsible for keeping Congress and other policy formulating agencies continually informed of lines of policy being developed elsewhere. This arrangement might be expected to result in some improvement over the present system though still more effective integration could, of course, be obtained if the proposed joint standing committee were given power to revise the decisions of these policy formulating agencies.

The establishment of such a committee was proposed by Professor Beard before the Progressive Conference in Washington,[8]

Functions," *Yale Law Journal*, XXVII, 892; Cecil T. Carr, *Delegated Legislation*, Ch. III; Herbert J. Friedman, "A Word about Commissions," *Harvard Law Review*, XXV, 710; Sharfman, I, 291. Professor John H. Wigmore is, perhaps, one of the most vigorous advocates in this country of delegations of this sort. Not only does he favor a much broader practice, but he even suggests a plan under which Congress would become a mere agent of the president, the head of the federal administration. See "Administration by the Executive vs. Administration by the Legislature," *Iowa Law Review*, XVIII, 205 ff. Some opposition to this practice is, of course, to be found. But it is based on emotional rather than practical considerations. See, for example, James M. Beck, *Our Wonderland of Bureaucracy*, ch. XII; Lord Gordon H. Hewart, *The New Despotism*, ch. IV.

[7] For instances where there has been a failure to co-ordinate see above pp. 56–57.

[8] See *New York Times*, March 12, 1931, p. 21.

although the proposal was not adopted by the conference in its final report.[9] Substantially the same kind of proposal was also made in the report of the Committee on Ministers' Powers of Great Britain.[10]

The second suggested improvement would be to require these commissions to hold, prior to their determinations of policy, general hearings, that is, hearings similar to those held by committees of Congress, to which any element of the public would have access. As it is now, the only hearing that they are required to hold resembles in all respects a judicial hearing where only parties directly affected by a proposed act of regulation have a right to be heard. So long as these commissions in the exercise of their judicial powers are expected to place particular emphasis upon the rights of individuals,[11] it would no doubt be desirable to continue to require this type of hearing. But, if they are also expected in their policy formulating and administrative powers to determine and represent the public interest, some additional and preliminary hearing of the type described would also seem to be desirable. In fact, such a hearing is indispensable if the public interest involved in their regulatory action is to be properly presented and properly considered.

The third suggested improvement would be for Congress to require these commissions insofar as practicable to formulate their

---

[9] *Ibid.*, March 13, 1931, p. 19.

[10] The committee differed from Professor Beard in suggesting the establishment of a committee for each house of Parliament rather than a joint committee. A proposal similar to Professor Beard's was made recently by the Select Committee on the Reorganization of the House of Representatives. See *H. R. Rep.* 4, 75th Cong., 1st sess., pp. 2–4.

[11] For there is room for difference of opinion concerning the way in which their judicial powers should be exercised. The state of Oregon has very definitely taken the position that the judicial powers of its Public Utilities Commissioner shall not be exercised with particular emphasis on the rights of individuals but rather as a means of furthering the public interest. See below p. 84.

policy by general rules or regulations instead of by a series of particular discretionary acts. In only a very few instances has it even empowered them to do this. The great bulk of their determinations of policy must, to have any legal character, be made in the form of particular acts of discretion or, since these commissions are exercising judicial power, in the very same act in which they determine the rights of particular individuals. This form of delegation is likely to have three possible consequences.

In the first place, in permitting a broad exercise of discretion where individual rights are being determined, it makes considerable discrimination possible among individuals with respect to their rights. This is Professor Freund's particular criticism of this form of delegation, and he suggests that insofar as possible these commissions formulate general rules for their own guidance.[12] These agencies might, of course, voluntarily do this. The Federal Trade Commission undertook something of this sort in its development of "Trade Practice Submittals."[13] But the practice could only be effectively established if they were required to do so.

In the second place, this form of delegation is likely to bring to these determinations of policy a very narrow view of the public interest. This is probable, not only because these commissions are not required to find some policy applicable to a group of individuals. It is also probable because, where the determinations are made in connection with the rights of particular individuals, the interest of the individual is brought to the forefront of the regulation and is likely to be overemphasized to the consequent neglect of the public interest.[14] It is even more probable because

[12] Ernst Freund, "The Substitution of Rule for Discretion," *American Political Science Review*, IX, 666.

[13] See Gerard C. Henderson, *The Federal Trade Commission*, pp. 78–82.

[14] See in this connection, Frederick F. Blachly and Miriam E. Oatman, *Administrative Legislation and Adjudication*, p. 51.

of the judicialized procedure they are required to observe,[15] although it might be offset in part by the requirement for a general hearing.

In the third place, the requirement that these commissions formulate their policy by specific acts of discretion is a direct encouragement to judicial review of the substance as well as of the application of governmental policy, since both substance and application are brought before the court as an inseparable act.[16] Admittedly there is still considerable disagreement whether the judiciary ought to maintain a power of review over the substance of this regulatory action, but it is important to note that this is one of the possible consequences of the form in which these delegations have been made.

It is, of course, still a question whether it would be practicable to require these commissions to formulate their policy by general regulation because of the variable and dynamic character of the situations they are seeking to regulate. But the large number of Trade Practice Submittals developed by the Federal Trade Commission, and the general regulations established by the late NRA, seem to indicate that there are definite possibilities in this form of delegation. But, even if it should be found impracticable for Congress to require these commissions to formulate public policy by general regulation—and this is a matter calling for special study—it would at least seem desirable for Congress to provide that they might function in this manner wherever possible and that such regulations would have the same legal standing as their specific orders.[17] To give these regulations a

---

[15] With the exception of the Board of Governors of the Federal Reserve System.

[16] For instances in which this effect seems to be especially noticeable, see, for example, *Interstate Commerce Commission* v. *Louisville and Nashville Railroad Co.*, 227 U. S. 88 (1913); *Federal Trade Commission* v. *Gratz*, 253 U. S. 421 (1920); *Crowell* v. *Benson*, 285 U. S. 22 (1932).

[17] A step in this direction was taken in 1934 in connection with the Securities

legal standing would not only be fairer to the individuals concerned but would probably make unnecessary a large number of specific orders. For the only stage at which individuals are now apprised of their rights is when specific orders are about to be issued.

The judicial powers, which most of these commissions are exercising in conjunction with administrative and in most cases also policy formulating powers, have caused greater concern and resulted in more prolific discussion than any phase of their action. In effect, this union of powers seems to represent an attempt by Congress to find in a single institution a certain compromise between the interests of the public and the interests of the individual. For on the one hand these commissions have the responsibility for representing the public interest in the exercise of their administrative powers, especially the power to initiate action, and in the exercise of their policy formulating powers, where such powers have also been entrusted to them. But on the other hand, in apparent deference to their judicial power, Congress has required them to proceed in the bulk of their action after the manner of a court.[18] In other words it has required them to proceed by a process of adjudication according to which individual rights are determined only after a formal notice and hearing and an opportunity to present evidence. They can thus be regarded as organs which are neither primarily responsible for representing the public interest nor primarily responsible for pro-

---

and Exchange Commission. See 48 Stat. L. 908, sec. 209(b) and the following discussion, Walter W. Cook, "Certainty in the Construction of the Law," *American Bar Association Journal*, XXI, 19–21.

[18] The Board of Governors of the Federal Reserve System which has very little judicial power is excepted, although it also is required to exercise in this manner such judicial power as it possesses. The ensuing discussion, therefore, only applies to a very limited extent to the Board of Governors. Moreover, the discussion does not apply to the Employees Compensation Commission since its judicial powers are not exercised in conjunction with its other powers.

tecting the interests of the individual. But they have clearly more responsibility for representing the public interest than the ordinary courts.

In contrasting these commissions with the courts, Mr. Gerard C. Henderson says:

> In a sense, of course, a court represents the public interest in administering a statute, but it has no continuing duty to see that the law is enforced. It is the court's duty to decide cases as they come before it, but if no indictment or civil action is brought, and the law becomes a dead letter, the court cannot be blamed. An administrative body on the other hand, has a continuing responsibility for results. It must ferret out violations, initiate proceedings, and adopt whatever proper methods are necessary to enforce compliance with the law.[19]

The present study makes no attempt to suggest at what point a compromise should be effected between the public interest and the interests of specific individuals: that is a matter for individual opinion. Instead it merely seeks to point out the specific proposals which have been made in connection with this exercise of judicial power and the practical aspects of the problem which those making these proposals generally neglect to consider.

Quite generally these proposals are founded on the assumption that the commissions will either disregard the interests of the individual and function only as organs of the public interest, or that they will, in any event, adequately safeguard the public interest. They naturally vary, however, in accordance with the conception held regarding the part that the public interest and the interests of the individual ought to play in the regulation undertaken.

At one extreme are those who place unusual emphasis upon the interests of the individual and accordingly propose that the or-

---

[19] *The Federal Trade Commission*, p. 91.

dinary judiciary, with its traditional solicitude for the position of the individual, should resume a rigid control over commission determinations. In opposing the passage of the Hepburn Act, under which Congress sought to accord greater finality to determinations of the Interstate Commerce Commission, Senator Foraker said:

> Why should this jurisdiction be withheld from the courts? Who distrusts them? Only violators of the law have ever had occasion to fear the justice they administer. They have been from the beginning of the common law the sure bulwark of the liberties and rights of the Anglo-Saxon race. Unmoved by passion, prejudice, or public clamor, they have ever been the steadying, reassuring factor in American government. Why should the advocates of this measure, affecting as it does the highest interests of the American people, seek to exclude them from their appropriate participation in the determination of the great questions that such legislation is sure to precipitate? That there is this unwillingness to allow the courts an unrestricted review is enough, not only to excite distrust of this remedy, but to condemn it.[20]

Whatever may be said for his position, Senator Foraker's proposal that the ordinary courts resume a rigid control over commission action is not above criticism as a practical step. For one of the principal causes of the courts' relaxation of control has been their actual inability to continue a rigid exercise of that control because of their long drawn out procedure, the present demands upon them, and their lack of experience in administration. Consequently, the proposals should be coupled with suggestions that would make the exercise of that control both possible and practical.

At the other extreme are those who in their emphasis upon the public interest either believe that these commissions should

---

[20] *Cong. Rec.*, 59th Cong., 1st sess., pp. 3117–18, cited in Dickinson, p. 74.

continue to enjoy their existing finality of decision or that their decisions should be given even greater finality. This group generally emphasizes the inefficiency of national regulation that otherwise would result. Thus Mr. Oscar L. Pond says in discussing the commission as a type of governmental institution:

The effectiveness of the orders of the commission . . . is largely determined by the conclusiveness of its findings. For the commission to be most efficient and of the greatest practical value, its orders and regulations, issued after due investigation, must become and remain effective with the final disposition of the commission. The necessary delays attending review by the courts and their lack of time and opportunity for investigating situations at first hand and as a current operating concern, constitute at once the occasion and the chief reason for commission control.[21]

Mr. William Z. Ripley takes the same position and offers practical evidence in its support. Speaking of the actual situation that existed in the field of railroad regulation while the courts maintained a rigid control over the action of the Interstate Commerce Commission, he says:

There was intolerable delay in the redress of grievances. . . . Intolerable delay in procedure was the constant complaint of shippers. Years elapsed before final judgments were rendered. The average duration of cases appealed was not less than four years. Sometimes they extended over twice that period. . . . The Georgia Railroad Commission cases were not settled for nine years. Nor did the tedious process end there. After the judicial review the entire question had to be remanded to the commission for a new order in conformity with the findings of the court. After nine years of litigation in the Chattanooga case, back it went to the Commission to be retried. First decided in 1892, it was reopened in 1904. Is it

---

[21] "Methods of Judicial Review in Relation to the Effectiveness of Commission Control," *Annals of the American Academy of Political and Social Science*, LIII, 60, cited in Dickinson, p. 71.

any wonder that the number of formal proceedings instituted by shippers steadily dwindled year by year? In 1901 only nineteen petitions were filed. Business of this sort was almost at a standstill.[22]

In between these two opposing groups stand those who concede that it would be undesirable to have the ordinary courts resume a rigid control over the action of these commissions, but who nevertheless believe that some greater security should be provided for the individual than now exists. Accordingly, this group suggests, either that some alteration for that purpose be effected within the commissions themselves, or that their judicial powers be entrusted to other agencies. The type of agencies suggested is one or more special administrative courts manned altogether or partly by officials who have had some practical experience or contact with the administrative side of government. These courts would function under a more simplified procedure than the ordinary courts.[23]

The only one thus far to suggest a mere alteration within the commissions themselves is Gerard C. Henderson. His suggestion is made only in connection with the Federal Trade Commis-

---

[22] *Railroad Rates and Regulation*, pp. 460–61, cited in Dickinson, p. 72, note 105. See also Dexter M. Keezer and Stacy May, *The Public Control of Business*, pp. 182–83, 237–38.

[23] For those favoring the creation of one or more special administrative courts, see: Blachly and Oatman, pp. 286–87; Benjamin Tuska, "Administrative Courts," *Constitutional Law Pamphlets*, I, 1–13; Marshall E. Dimock, "Special Courts for Administrative Cases," *National Municipal Review*, XX, 691–93; William J. Donovan, "The Need for a Commerce Court," *Annals of the American Academy of Political and Social Science*, CXLVII, 138–45; James Hart, "The President and Federal Administration," in *Essays on the Law and Practice of Governmental Administration—A Volume in Honor of Frank Johnson Goodnow*, p. 93; Herbert Corey, "Trial by Commission," *Nation's Business*, XXV (Feb., 1937), 29. Recently a bill to create a special administrative court reached the committee stage. See *Hearings before a Subcommittee on the Judiciary of the Senate on S. 3676*, 75th Cong., 3rd sess.

sion, but it is also applicable to the others. He believes that the Federal Trade Commission should and could be made more judicially minded; and he accordingly suggests that it merely make inquiries into business practices deemed to be unfair and that the responsibility for instituting legal proceedings be left to private individuals.[24] Mr. Henderson, of course, sees one probable objection to this proposal—namely, that private individuals could not be expected to represent fully the public interest actually involved in the proceeding. He therefore suggests that the commission's counsel be permitted to present further testimony, though he is careful to add that the officer should not appear in a prosecuting capacity but "merely to make sure that the facts were fully developed and that expert impartial testimony was available." [25]

One of the principal factors in the problem presented by this exercise of judicial power in the manner provided is frequently overlooked by those making the specific proposals noted.[26] The assumption is quite generally made that the policy formulating and administrative responsibilities of these commissions will always eclipse their judicial responsibilities with the result that they will always give controlling or at least adequate consideration to the public interest. But it is equally probable that the reverse situation may at times result with a consequent disregard for the public interest. This is especially probable, since their judicial responsibility has been impressed upon them by the requirement that they observe in the bulk of their action a judicialized form of procedure.[27]

In 1925, Mr. John Bauer claimed that such a situation had

---

[24] *The Federal Trade Commission*, p. 329.

[25] *Ibid.*

[26] With the exception of Hart, Blachly and Oatman, and Corey.

[27] This requirement for a judicialized procedure, moreover, has been very strictly enforced by the courts. See *U. S.* v. *Abilene Ry. Co.*, 265 U. S. 274 (1924); *I. C. C.* v. *Louisville and Nashville Ry. Co.*, 227 U. S. 88 (1913).

arisen among state public utility commissions with a resulting lack of vigor on behalf of the public interest. According to Mr. Bauer:

> A commission which must sit in a judicial capacity cannot readily be unflinching in its duties to the public to obtain the lowest possible rates. There is little doubt that this has caused the commission to avoid the facing of perplexing responsibilities. On the public side, the commissions have avoided the starting of rate investigations as long as they could. Even if the facts justified a reduction in rates and were known to the experts, the tendency has been strong to do nothing until an active public insistence forced an investigation. . . . The responsibility for changes, therefore, has rested practically upon the initiative of public officials and of the companies who could represent the public and the investors without judicial restraints.[28]

Mr. Bauer accordingly suggests that the legislatures define more specific policies for the commissions, thus making their work, as he contends, "practically automatic and their procedure almost altogether administrative."[29]   This suggestion, however, that the legislature undertake a more detailed formulation of policy, encounters the practical objections noted in the earlier part of this chapter.[30]

In 1931, the existence of the same condition noted by Mr. Bauer became so apparent in the state of Oregon as to lead to definite action with respect to its Public Service Commission. In that year the state abolished the commission and substituted a Public Utilities Commissioner; and, while the new law provides that the commissioner may issue his orders after a judicial procedure, it does not require him to observe that form of procedure. It specifically authorizes him to issue these orders after investigation only and provides that such orders shall have the same legal

---

[28] *Effective Regulation of Public Utilities*, p. 359.   See also William E. Mosher and Finla G. Crawford, *Public Utility Regulation*, pp. 34–40.

[29] Bauer, p. 360.   [30] See above, pp. 71–72.

effect as orders issued after a judicial procedure.[31] Further, and
equally important, since the commissioner might still be influenced by the judicial character of his tasks, involving as they
do power to determine with considerable finality the rights of
particular individuals, the new law leaves no doubt that furtherance of the public interest is to be the paramount responsibility
of the commissioner.

In the words of the statute, "It shall be his duty to represent the
patrons, users of the service, and consumers of the product, of
any public utility, and the public generally in all controversies
respecting rates, charges . . . and all matters of which he has
jurisdiction, and in respect thereof it shall be his duty to make use
of the jurisdiction and powers of his office to protect such patrons,
users and consumers, and the public generally." [32] No such clear
mandate exists in the statutory provisions relating to federal commissions.

More recently, and with specific reference to federal commissions, Dr. James Hart called attention to the possibility of this
condition in the following passage:

> There is a latent ambiguity in the very purpose for which our
> regulatory commissions have been set up. This becomes apparent as
> soon as it is realized that discretionary choice is involved. An ad-
> ministrative tribunal is at once a regulatory and a judicial organ.
> Its *raison d'être* is to protect a public interest by the control of
> special groups, but its procedure involves a judicial hearing. If
> the tribunal regards itself as representative of the public, it becomes
> at the hearing both judge and advocate, and in its decision primarily
> the advocate. The hearing becomes merely the presentation of
> factors which it must consider, and ceases to be a judicial hearing
> except in form. On the other hand, if the tribunal regards itself
> primarily as a court which is bound to base its decisions upon an

---

[31] Oregon Laws (1931), ch. 103, sec. 6, revising Oregon Code (1930), sec.
61–245.   [32] *Ibid.*, sec. 5.

impartial examination of the arguments of counsel, it is apt to lose sight of its main function.[33]

Dr. Hart accordingly proposes the abolition of these commissions and the delegation of their administrative and policy formulating powers to purely administrative officials and of their judicial powers to administrative courts.[34]

Still more recently the Federal Council for Industrial Progress, in its study of the administration of the Federal Trade Commission Act, has unanimously recommended a divorce between the judicial and other powers of the Federal Trade Commission. In this connection the committee says:

The functions of the Federal Trade Commission, if that body be continued, should be limited to those of investigation and prosecution. Because of disadvantages in vesting in one body both administrative and judicial functions, the judicial functions of the Federal Trade Commission should be transferred to an independent commission. This commission preferably should include in its personnel, besides incumbents with legal training, lay representatives of industry, labor, and the consuming public and should have jurisdiction, but not to the exclusion of the courts, in cases instituted either by the Federal Trade Commission or by aggrieved parties.[35]

Over the final nature of specific institutional arrangements opinion may well vary in accordance with the particular emphasis

[33] "The President and Federal Administration" in *Essays on the Law and Practice of Governmental Administration*, p. 75. See also Blachly and Oatman, p. 239.

[34] *Op. cit.*, p. 93. A substantially similar proposal is also made by Blachly and Oatman, pp. 286–87.

[35] Council for Industrial Progress, *Reports of Committees and Resolutions Adopted March 12, 1936* (submitted to the Co-ordinator for Industrial Co-operation), p. 36. In his recent study for the President's Committee on Administrative Management, Professor Cushman makes a somewhat similar proposal. See *The Problem of the Independent Regulatory Commissions*, published by the President's Committee on Administrative Management, January, 1937.

upon the public interest and the interests of the individual. Thus, while Dr. Hart shows sufficient concern for the interests of the individual to propose the establishment of administrative courts for his protection, the state of Oregon made no provision for that purpose, even though it made a judicial procedure optional with the commissioner in the exercise of his judicial powers and further made it clear that his paramount responsibility was to represent the public interest. In effect, the state of Oregon has taken the position that the judicial powers of its Public Utilities Commissioner shall be primarily exercised as a means of furthering the public interest or with primary emphasis on the public interest. But there would seem to be little doubt that the attempt to entrust to a single agency the two-fold responsibility for furthering the public interest and protecting the interest of the individual is not conducive to the most effective fulfillment of either responsibility.[36]

One other aspect of the problem presented by this commission exercise of judicial power, though of particular concern only where some further form of judicial control is desired, relates to the kind of protection that ought to be accorded the individual. Should the control be designed to secure certain substantive rights for the individual or merely to protect him from discrimination, intentional or unintentional? In general, those who advocate control by administrative courts favor securing certain substantive rights for the individual. Thus, they generally speak of the

---

[36] The foregoing discussion does not apply to the Employees Compensation Commission. The commission is exercising its judicial powers independently of its administrative powers and there would seem little question that, in the exercise of its judicial power of deciding compensation claims presented by individuals, the interest of the individual should receive dominant consideration. The public has little interest in such determinations. However, from the standpoint of organization, the administrative powers of the commission could be more effectively exercised, it would seem, by a subordinate single head agency.

added efficiency of regulation that will result if that regulation is to be controlled by a court composed of men with some administrative experience. It is undoubtedly true that more effective regulation will result where control is exercised by an administrative court in place of the ordinary courts. But it has not been sufficiently emphasized that any form of substantive control involves a participation in the actual formulation of policy with an inevitable duality and inconsistency of approach in the treatment of national problems.

On the other hand a few of those who favor the creation of administrative courts, as James Hart, Frederick F. Blachly, and Miriam E. Oatman, apparently do not believe that the administrative courts should be given any substantive control.[37] In actual practice, however, it would be difficult to prevent the administrative courts from constantly encroaching upon the field of public policy so long as the practice is continued of formulating policy by specific order, that is, formulating and executing policy in one and the same act. This point was earlier discussed as an argument for the requirement that these commissions formulate their policy by general regulations insofar as possible.[38]

---

[37] Hart, *op. cit.*, p. 79; Blachly and Oatman, p. 287. For recent congressional hearings on a bill to establish administrative courts, see *Hearings before a Subcommittee on the Judiciary of the Senate on S. 3676*, 75th Cong., 3rd sess.

[38] See above p. 76.

CHAPTER FIVE

Suggested Changes for More Effective Administrative Technique

IN THE course of this study certain fairly distinct uses of the independent commission were pointed out and certain broad institutional characteristics common to all or most of them discussed. Attention was first directed to their actual position of independence, and the general conclusion was drawn that they are not in a position to attain the fullest measure of independence in fact until the following steps are taken: (1) elimination of the uncertainty that now exists concerning the actual security of their members against the president's coercive use of the removal power, (2) provision for much longer terms of office, and (3) elimination of the bipartisan provisions which are found in connection with all but the Board of Governors of the Federal Reserve System. At the same time the discussion showed that these agencies are far from being completely or effectively subject to presidential direction.

Attention was then turned to the desirability of independence and also board control, and an analysis of these principles of organization attempted in terms of the powers being exercised by all or some of these commissions, namely, administrative, policy formulating, and judicial powers. On the basis of analysis and very limited experimentation it was suggested that subordination and single head control would be likely to result in a more effective performance of their administrative [1] and policy formulating powers and of their judicial powers, unless the judicial powers are to be exercised with particular emphasis on the rights of the individual. If these powers are to be so exercised, it was suggested that they be separated from the other powers so that the appropriate principles of organization might be applied. The same suggestion in regard to separation was also made in a later discussion of the conflicting responsibilities imposed upon these commissions, provided again they are expected to exercise their judicial powers with particular emphasis on the rights of the individual.

Attention was then directed to the combination or union of powers represented in the work of these commissions and the accompanying procedural requirements. In discussing the union between policy formulating and administrative powers, the position was taken that, while this union of powers seems indispensable to intelligent governmental action, certain improvements can be made in the present manner in which the policy formulating powers are being exercised. Three improvements were suggested. The first, based on the need for greater integration in policy formulation and a suggestion that was also made in another connection, is to subordinate to the president in tenure and decision the members of the commissions entrusted with this power. Pending such a step it was suggested that Congress establish a joint standing committee with at least the responsibility of keeping Congress and all policy formulating units continually informed of the various lines of policy being developed elsewhere. The second suggestion is to require these commissions when exercising their policy formulating powers to hold general hearings similar to those held by Congress, where any element of

---

[1] Except perhaps the investigative function of the United States Tariff Commission.

the public with a reasonable interest in the proceeding would have a right to be heard and a right to submit evidence. The third suggestion is to require insofar as practicable that policy be formulated by general regulations rather than by particular acts of discretion.

In discussing the union between judicial powers, on the one hand, and administrative and, in most cases, policy formulating powers on the other hand, two alternative suggestions were made. The first is to effect an institutional separation in the exercise of the judicial and other powers, entrusting the judicial powers to administrative courts. The second is to provide that the judicial powers shall merely be exercised in furtherance of, or with primary emphasis on, the public interest, and, in furtherance of this end, to eliminate the present requirements for a judicialized procedure. The choice will depend upon the emphasis to be placed on the public interest and the interest of the individual, but either alternative would seem to constitute an improvement over the present arrangement where the commissions are apparently expected to place particular emphasis on both sets of interests.

In conclusion, it seems advisable to apply more specifically the various suggestions that have been made. The same suggestions are made for the following commissions: the Interstate Commerce Commission, the Federal Communications Commission, the Securities and Exchange Commission, the Federal Power Commission, the Federal Trade Commission, the National Bituminous Coal Commission,* and the United States Maritime Commission. These suggestions are:

1. Reorganize them as subordinate single head units within the appropriate federal executive departments.

2. Require them when exercising their policy formulating powers to hold general hearings, similar to those held by committees of Congress, where any element of the public with a

---

* See note p. 5.

reasonable interest in the proceedings would have a right to be heard and a right to present evidence.

3. Require them insofar as possible to exercise their policy formulating powers in the form of general regulations instead of specific orders.

4. Either entrust their judicial powers to administrative courts or provide that these powers shall be exercised in furtherance of, or with primary emphasis on, the public interest, and eliminate the present requirements for a judicialized procedure.

For the Board of Governors of the Federal Reserve System the same suggestions are made except the requirement that policy be formulated by general regulation, since most of the policy formulating powers of the board are now being exercised in this manner.

For the Social Security Board * and the National Mediation Board, which are only exercising administrative powers, the only suggestion is to reorganize them as subordinate single head agencies within the appropriate federal executive departments.

For the United States Tariff Commission, which is also only exercising administrative powers, no suggestion is made, except, perhaps, to make it definitely independent, if possible, and closely supervise results.

For the National Labor Relations Board the following suggestions are made:

1. Reorganize it as a subordinate single head agency within the appropriate federal executive department.

2. Either entrust its judicial power to an administrative court or provide that this power shall be exercised in furtherance of, or with primary emphasis on, the public interest, and eliminate the present requirement for a judicialized procedure.[2]

---

[2] The second alternative would not seem desirable, however, unless a change is made in the present law which seems to make the board the representative of the employees only. But it may be expected that such a one-sided law will be changed in the near future.

* See note p. 5.

Finally, for the Employees Compensation Commission the following suggestions are made:

1. Reorganize it as a subordinate single head agency within the appropriate federal executive department.

2. Entrust its judicial power to an administrative court or possibly the existing Court of Claims. The alternative suggestion that has been made in connection with the judicial powers of the other commissions would hardly be appropriate for the exercise of these judicial powers. For they consist of hearing and deciding compensation claims presented by individuals, and the public would seem to have little real interest in such decisions.

If there has been any general theme running through this entire work, it is the necessity for intelligent experimentation with administrative techniques, that is, experimentation accompanied by supervision or continuous and close observation by an agency of the government which is in a position to observe. It is hoped, therefore, that if Congress decides to experiment along the lines suggested or other lines, it will at the same time provide for supervision of the experiments. Indeed, it would even be desirable, in the opinion of the author, for Congress to establish a permanent agency with the sole responsibility of supervising all experiments and for continuously investigating the possibilities of new and improved administrative techniques.

Selected Bibliography

I. PRIMARY MATERIAL

United States

Board of Mediation. *Annual Report*, 1933.

Bureau of Animal Industry. *Annual Reports*, 1928–1938; *Dockets*, 311, 314.

Code, 1934 and supplements.

Commission on Industrial Relations. *Final Report, Sen. Doc.* 415, Vol. I, 64th Cong., 1st sess.

Commissioner of Mediation. *Report on the Operations of the United States Board of Mediation and Conciliation*, 1919.

Congress. *Congressional Record*, 59th Cong., 1st sess.; 63rd Cong., 2nd sess.; 64th Cong., 1st sess.; 66th Cong., 3rd sess.; 67th Cong., 1st sess.; 69th Cong., 1st sess.; 70th Cong., 1st sess.; 71st Cong., 2nd sess.; 75th Cong., 1st sess.; 75th Cong., 2nd sess.; 75th Cong., 3rd sess.

—— *Hearings before the Joint Committee on Government Organization*, 75th Cong., 1st sess.

—— *Hearings before the Joint Committee on the Reorganization of the Executive Departments*, 68th Cong., 1st sess.

—— *Report of the Joint Committee on Agricultural Inquiry*, H. R. Rep. 408, Vol. III, Part 3, Ch. I, 67th Cong., 1st sess.

—— *Report of the Joint Committee on the Reorganization of the Executive Departments*, H. R. Doc. 356, 68th Cong., 1st sess.

House of Representatives. *H. R. Rep.* 4, 75th Cong., 1st sess.;

H. R. Rep. 248, 67th Cong., 1st sess.; *H. R. Rep.* 533, 63rd Cong., 2nd sess.; *H. R. Rep.* 615, 74th Cong., 1st sess.; *H. R. Rep.* 678, 64th Cong., 1st sess.; *H. R. Rep.* 1383, 73rd Cong., 2nd sess.; *H. R. Rep.* 1487, 75th Cong., 1st sess.

Senate. *Hearings before the Select Committee on Government Organization,* 75th Cong., 1st sess.; *Hearings before a Subcommittee on the Judiciary of the Senate on S. 3676,* 75th Cong.; 3rd sess.; *Sen. Rep.* 1236, 75th Cong., 3rd (*sic* 1st) sess.

Council for Industrial Progress. *Reports of Committees and Resolutions Adopted March 12, 1936.*

Department of Agriculture. *Annual Reports, 1928–1938.*

Department of Labor. *Annual Reports,* 1921, 1933.

Federal Trade Commission. *Annual Reports,* 1925, 1926.

President's Committee on Administrative Management. *The Exercise of Rule-Making Power and the Preparation of Proposed Legislative Measures by Administrative Departments,* prepared by James Hart and Edwin E. Witte, January, 1937.

—— *The Problem of the Independent Regulatory Commissions,* prepared by Robert E. Cushman, January, 1937.

Statutes at Large.

Supreme Court Reports.

Tariff Commission. *Annual Reports,* 1922, 1927, 1929, 1930.

California

Final Report of the Fact-Finding Committee of the Senate, 1933. Political Code, 1931.

Iowa

Institute for Government Research of the Brookings Institution. *A Survey of Administration in Iowa,* 1933.

Mississippi

Institute for Government Research of the Brookings Institution.

Report on a Survey of the Organization and Administration of State and County Government in Mississippi, 1932.
—— *Summary of the Facts, Findings and Recommendations of a Report on a Survey of State and County Government in Mississippi, 1932.*

Ohio

Joint Committee on Economy in the Public Service. *Report, 1929.*
Report on a Summary of Recommendations for the Administrative Reorganization of Ohio's State Government, 1920. Prepared by Don C. Sowers.

Oregon

Code, 1930.
Governor. *Inaugural Message of Julius L. Meier, Governor of Oregon, to the Thirty-Sixth Legislative Assembly, 1931.*
—— *Message of Walter M. Pierce, Governor of Oregon, to the Thirty-First Legislative Assembly, 1925.*
Laws.
Public Utilities Commissioner of Oregon. *Report, 1935.*

Great Britain

Committee on Ministers' Powers of Great Britain. *Report presented by the Lord High Chancellor to Parliament,* April, 1932, London, England.

II. Secondary Material

Albertsworth, E. F. "The Federal Supreme Court and Industrial Development." *American Bar Association Journal,* XVI (May, 1930), 317.
Barnett, George A. and McCabe, David. *Mediation, Investigation and Arbitration in Industrial Disputes.* New York, 1916.
Bauer, John. *Effective Regulation of Public Utilities.* New York: The Macmillan Co., 1925.
Beard, Charles A. and William. *The American Leviathan.* New York, 1930.

Beck, James M. *Our Wonderland of Bureaucracy.* New York, 1932.

Blachly, Frederick F. and Oatman, Miriam E. *Administrative Legis-lation and Adjudication.* Washington, 1934.

Blaisdell, Thomas C. *The Federal Trade Commission.* New York: Columbia University Press, 1932.

Brayman, Harold. "The FPC, the FCC, the SEC," *Public Utilities Fortnightly,* XVIII (July, 1936), 115.

Bruner, Felix. "Trial without Jury," *Nation's Business,* XXV (January, 1937), 35.

Buck, Arthur E. *Administrative Consolidation in State Govern-ments.* New York, 1930.

Bunbury, H. N. "The Economic Regulation of Public Utilities," *Public Administration,* IV (July, 1926), 208.

Caldwell, O. H. "The Administration of Federal Radio Legisla-tion," *Annals of the American Academy of Political and Social Science,* CXLII (supp.) (March, 1929), 45.

Carr, Cecil T. *Delegated Legislation.* Cambridge, England, 1921.

Cheadle, John B. "The Delegation of Legislative Functions," *Yale Law Journal,* XXVII (May, 1918), 892.

Cleveland, Frederick A. "The Reorganization of the Federal Gov-ernment," *Proceedings of the American Academy of Political Science,* IX (July, 1921), 361.

Comer, John P. *Legislative Functions of National Administrative Authorities.* New York and London, 1927.

Commission of Inquiry on Public Service Personnel. *Better Gov-ernment Personnel.* Washington, 1935.

—— *Minutes of Evidence.* New York, 1935.

Cook, Walter W. "Certainty in the Construction of the Law," *American Bar Association Journal,* XXI (January, 1935), 19.

Cooper, Robert M. "Administrative Justice and the Role of Dis-cretion," *Yale Law Journal,* XLVII (February, 1938), 577.

Corey, Herbert. "Trial by Commission," *Nation's Business,* XXV (February, 1937), 29.

Davis, D. W. "How Administrative Control is Working in Idaho," *National Municipal Review,* VIII (November, 1919), 615.

Dickinson, John. *Administrative Justice and the Supremacy of the Law*. Cambridge, 1927.

Dimock, Marshall E. *British Public Utilities and National Development*. London, 1933.

—— "The Prospect for Administrative Tribunals," *California Law Review*, XX (January, 1932), 162.

—— "Special Courts for Administrative Cases," *National Municipal Review*, XX (December, 1931), 691.

Dodd, Walter F. "Reorganizing State Government," *Annals of the American Academy of Political and Social Science*, CXIII (May, 1924), 161.

Donovan, William J. "The Need for a Commerce Court," *Annals of the American Academy of Political and Social Science*, CXLVII (January, 1930), 138.

Eastman, Joseph B. "The Place of the Independent Commission," *Constitutional Review*, XII (April, 1928), 95.

Ellis, Howell. "Four Reasons Why I Question the One-man Commission Idea," *Public Utilities Fortnightly*, IX (February, 1932), 155.

Frankfurter, Felix. *The Public and Its Government*. New Haven, 1930.

Freund, Ernst. *Administrative Powers over Persons and Property*. Chicago, 1928.

—— "The Substitution of Rule for Discretion in Public Law," *American Political Science Review*, IX (November, 1915), 666.

Friedman, Herbert J. "A Word about Commissions," *Harvard Law Review*, XXV (June, 1912), 704.

Friedrich, Carl J. "Responsible Government Service under the American Constitution," in *Problems of the American Public Service*. New York: McGraw-Hill Book Co., Inc., 1935.

Gaus, John M. "The New Problem of Administration," *Minnesota Law Review*, VIII (February, 1924), 217.

Goodnow, Frank J. *Principles of the Administrative Law of the United States*. New York and London, 1905.

Gregory, T. E. G. *Tariffs—A Study of Method*. London, 1921.

Hart, James. "The Bearing of Myers v. United States upon the Independence of Federal Administrative Tribunals," *American Political Science Review*, XXII (August, 1929), 657.

—— "The President and Federal Administration," in *Essays on the Law and Practice of Governmental Administration—A Volume in Honor of Frank Johnson Goodnow*. Baltimore: Johns Hopkins Press, 1935.

—— *Tenure of Office under the Constitution*. Baltimore, 1930.

Henderson, Gerard C. *The Federal Trade Commission*. New Haven: Yale University Press, 1924.

Herring, E. Pendleton. *Federal Commissioners—A Study of Their Careers and Qualifications*. Cambridge: Harvard University Press, 1936.

—— "The Federal Power Commission and the Power of Politics," *Public Utilities Fortnightly*, XV (February and March, 1935), 223, 292.

—— "Politics, Personalities and the Federal Trade Commission," *American Political Science Review*, XXIX (February, 1935), 32.

—— Public Administration and the Public Interest. New York and London, 1936.

Hewart, Lord Gordon H. *The New Despotism*. New York and London, 1929.

Holcombe, Arthur N. "Administrative Reorganization in the Federal Government," *Annals of the American Academy of Political and Social Science*, XCV (May, 1921), 242.

Institute for Government Research of the Brookings Institution. Monographs nos. 5, 7, 12, 17, 18, 20, 65.

Keezer, Dexter M. and May, Stacy. *The Public Control of Business*. New York and London, 1930.

Laski, Harold J. *A Grammar of Politics*. New Haven, 1926.

Locklin, Philip D. *Railroad Regulation since 1920*. London, 1928.

Lowden, Frank O. "Business Government," *Saturday Evening Post*, March 14, 1920.

Mathews, John M. *The American Constitutional System*. New York and London, 1932.

—— *The Principles of American State Administration.* New York and London, 1917.

—— "State Administrative Reorganization," *American Political Science Review,* XVI (August, 1922), 387.

Mayers, Lewis. *The Federal Service.* New York and London, 1922.

Morganston, Charles E. *The Appointing and Removal Power of the President of the United States.* Washington, 1929.

Mosher, William E. and Crawford, Finla G. *Public Utility Regulation.* New York and London, 1933.

National Budget Committee of New York City, "Proposed Reorganization of the Federal Executive Departments," printed in *New York Times,* June 14, 1921.

Nation's Business, editorial entitled, "A New Spirit in Federal Trade Cases," XV (July, 1927), 30.

Needham, Charles W. "Judicial Determinations by Administrative Commissions," *American Political Science Review,* X (May, 1916), 235.

Page, Thomas W. *Making the Tariff in the United States.* New York, 1924.

Pond, Oscar L. "Methods of Judicial Review in Relation to the Effectiveness of Commission Control," *Annals of the American Academy of Political and Social Science,* LIII (May, 1914), 54.

Ripley, William Z. *Railroad Rates and Regulation.* 2d ed. New York: Longmans, Green and Co., Inc., 1913.

Sharfman, Isaiah L. *The Interstate Commerce Commission.* Parts I–IV. New York: Commonwealth Fund, 1931–1937.

Spicer, George W. "Proposed Plan for Administrative Reorganization for Oklahoma," *National Municipal Review,* XIX (May, 1930), 308.

Spurr, Henry C. *Guiding Principles of Public Service Regulation.* Vol. I. Rochester and Washington, 1924.

Stafford, Paul T. "The New Amateur in Public Administration," *American Political Science Review,* XXIX (February, 1935), 258.

Tuska, Benjamin. "Administrative Courts," *Constitutional Law Pamphlets,* I (October, 1926), 1.

Watkins, Myron W. "The Federal Trade Commission; A Critical Survey," *Quarterly Journal of Economics*, XL (August, 1926), 561.

West, Oswald. "Oregon's Unique Experiment with a One-man Utility Commission," *Public Utilities Fortnightly*, VII (April, 1931), 542.

Weyforth, William O. *The Federal Reserve Board*. Baltimore, 1933.

Wheeler, Burton K. "I. C. C. Should be Independent," *Railway Age*, CII (April 10, 1937), 631.

White, Leonard D. *Introduction to the Study of Public Administration*. New York, 1926.

Wigmore, John H. "Administration by the Executive vs. Administration by the Legislature," *Iowa Law Review*, XVIII (January, 1933), 198.

Willoughby, Westel W. *The Constitutional Law of the United States*. 2d ed. Vol. III. New York, 1929.

Willoughby, William F. *Legal Status and Functions of the General Accounting Office of the National Government*. Baltimore, 1927.

—— *The Principles of Public Administration*. Baltimore, 1927.

Wilmerding, Lucius. *Government by Merit*. New York, 1935.

Witte, Edwin C. *The Government in Labor Disputes*. New York and London, 1932.

III. Special Bibliographies

International Labor Office. *Conciliation and Arbitration in Industrial Disputes*. Series (a) no. 34. Geneva, 1933.

U. S. Tariff Commission. *The Tariff—A Bibliography*. Washington, 1934.

Table of Cases

State v. *Henry*, 60 Fla. 246; 53 S. Rep. 742 (1910).

State ex rel. Meader v. *Sullivan*, 58 Ohio St. 504; 51 N. E. Rep. 48 (1898).

State v. *Wilson*, 121 N. C. 425; 28 S. E. Rep. 554 (1897).

U. S. v. *Abilene Ry. Co.*, 265 U. S. 274 (1924).

U. S. v. *Germaine*, 99 U. S. 508 (1879).

U. S. v. *Perkins*, 116 U. S. 483 (1885).

Wilcox v. *People*, 90 Ill. 186 (1878).

Index